Arts Beat
The Arts in Victoria

ARTS BEAT

THE ARTS IN VICTORIA

BY AUDREY ST. DENYS JOHNSON
EDITED BY R.DALE MCINTOSH

Cover design by Terry Gallagher/Doowah Design
Author photo by Alex Barta, Victoria *Times-Colonist*

Published with the assistance of The Canada Council.

Printed and bound in Canada by Hignell Printing Ltd.

Proceeds from the sale of this book will be used to create a
scholarship in Audrey Johnson's memory at the
University of Victoria.

Canadian Cataloguing in Publication Data

Johnson, Audrey St. Denys.
    Arts Beat

        Includes bibliographical references and index.
        ISBN 1-896239-06-4

1. Arts–British Columbia–Victoria–History. 2. Victoria (B.C.)–
Intellectual Life. I. Title
NX513.V6J64 1995   700'.9711'28   C95-910847-5

(Alex Barta, Victoria *Times-Colonist*)

Audrey St. Denys Johnson (1915–1993)

Table of Contents

Foreword (by Mavor Moore) v
Introduction (by the editor) vii
Acknowledgements xii

Part I — A Road Taken
  1: City of Dreams 3
  2: Early Experiences in the Arts 9
  3: Getting from A to B with No Easy Lessons 20
  4: New Directions and Responsibilities 31

Part II — Curtains Rising
  5: The Altar of St. Cecilia 37
  6: Orchestras 47
  7: Victoria Conservatory of Music 64
     Photographs (series a)
  8: Music Festivals 71
  9: Music Theatre and Pacific Opera Victoria 77
 10: Curtains Rose and Fell 96
 11: The Victoria Theatre Guild 104
 12: Early Professional Theatre 117
     Photographs (series b)
 13: The McPherson Playhouse 123
 14: The Bastion Theatre 130
 15: The Phoenix 146
 16: The Belfry Theatre 162
 17: Kaleidoscope Theatre 172
 18: The Art Gallery of Greater Victoria 179

Epilogue 195
Index of Names 197

Audrey's contributions to the arts were absolutely stellar and Trojan. She was a very honest critic and mentor.
— Patricia Bovey

I admired Audrey's integrity, honesty, a sense of humour that didn't always find its way into her often charitable reviews, her liberalism, and an infectious love of life — she was a five star lady.
— Michæl D. Reid

Audrey was one of the few critics who understood what live entertainment was all about and she cared deeply about the welfare and success of every company and artist in our community. Her enthusiasm, however, seldom blinded her to our shortcomings.
— Peter Mannering

Audrey championed the view that neither man nor the society he inhabits can ever live by bread alone. She never gave up her crusade for the arts, whatever the discouragements, and what we now enjoy is infinitely stronger and richer because of her.
— Hugh R. Stephen

Audrey was a steadfast supporter of the arts.
— Timothy Vernon

Audrey played a vital role in starting and continually supporting the Victoria Sumphony, the local music festival, the summer drama festival, and the Conservatory of Music. She was fiercely dedicated to encouraging young artists in all the arts.
— Helen Smith

Foreword

I met Audrey Johnson in January, 1964, when I presented the topical revue *Spring Thaw* in Victoria's Royal Theatre, opening its first cross-country tour, and she reviewed it for the *Daily Times*. We could not have had a happier introduction. It was not only that she adored the show, and that as a former newspaper critic myself I appreciated her warm response; what endeared her to me was less the praise than the thoroughly unconventional demur that preceded it:

> I give up. I apologize. I have been conquered — or thawed! Having just been exposed to the sizzling barbs of *Spring Thaw*, I abjectly admit that I goofed in my recent allegations that the Canadian nation as a whole suffers from an inferiority complex. No people that can produce such a merciless peepshow on their own shortcomings...could possibly have an inferiority complex.

There are very few critics anywhere generous enough to begin with an apology, and I therefore paid uncommon heed to the rest of what Audrey Johnson had to say. I have continued to do so for thirty years — especially after we moved from Toronto to Canada's west coast in 1984 and were able to renew the friendship in person.

For an appreciation of what was happening in the arts in British Columbia, and particularly in Victoria, I have relied greatly on her rare knowledge and wisdom. The serious dearth of cultural history texts in this country, only now being repaired by arts scholars and teachers such as Dale McIntosh, has contributed to our appalling national amnesia. We must be grateful to Audrey's husband Maurice, and to editor McIntosh, for making available to future generations these rich reminiscences of a life spent in observing and analysing arts activities in one of Canada's oldest, most distinctive and fascinating cities.

But perhaps Audrey Johnson's most significant legacy lies in the very artistic sophistication now taken for granted in her (now my) home town. Far from being merely a parochial enthusiast or gadfly, she was *au courant* with what was happening in theatre, music, literature, and visual art across Canada and in the wider world. In short, she was able to put both local and visiting activities into a larger context for her readers — a service that I consider the first of critical responsibilities. She continues to do so in this valuable book.

— Mavor Moore

Introduction

When Audrey Johnson retired in 1987 from 51 years' association with the Victoria *Times* and later the *Times-Colonist* she began writing a manuscript on arts development in Victoria. For background information she relied both on memories of her own personal experiences with the arts as well as the vast number of columns, articles, and reviews she had written over those years. When she died on 12 August 1993, the manuscript was about 80 per cent completed. Because of my background in historical aspects of the arts in Victoria,[1] I was asked by her husband, Maurice, to edit and subsequently complete the manuscript. This was a challenge which I was happy to accept, since it not only completes Audrey's story — which is, in essence, memoirs of the arts in Victoria from the 1930s to the 1990s — but rounds out my own research, which extends back to 1850. For both of us it is a kind of "rounding out," although Audrey's memoirs are much anecdotally richer than the sometimes stale facts with which I have worked for the past 20 years — for she lived everything she wrote here.

Audrey was born on 21 December 1915, in Toronto, the daughter of Sidney and Florence Wood. Mr. Wood was a banker and had come to Toronto with his wife from South Africa shortly before Audrey's birth. Soon after Audrey was born the family was posted to Winnipeg and it was there that Audrey began her first musical studies. In 1920 the Woods came to Victoria and here Audrey completed the bulk of her education, including piano studies with one of Victoria's most outstanding teacher of piano of the time,

---

1 Published works include: *A Documentary History of Music in Victoria, British Columbia: Volume I – 1850–1899* (1982) and Volume II – 1900–1950 (1994), *History of Music in British Columbia* (1989), and *One Hundred Years of Singing: The Arion Male Voice Choir* (1992) as well as several articles.

Stanley Shale, with whom she gained the Licentiate of the Royal Schools of Music (LRSM).

Audrey was only 17 when tragedy struck.[2] Her father died of cancer on 15 January 1933 leaving the family to cope in the midst of one of the worst economic depressions ever to hit Canada. It was then that Audrey's dreams of becoming an artist, or a musician, or a writer seemed to be dashed — she felt she must immediately seek gainful employment if the family were to survive.

She began by using the skills imparted to her by Stanley Shale (and before him Kate Webb) by teaching piano in her home while completing a business course and attempting to keep the beginning fragments of a potential career in the arts alive. The latter involved spending all her free time either writing poetry, some of which was published, engaging in her passions for block printing and watercolour, or reviewing books for the Victoria *Times*. While she got no remuneration for her reviews she was allowed to keep the books!

More than anything, Audrey loved to go to concerts and plays but, with limited financial resources and even less free time, she found this difficult. She religiously read the reviews of all concerts written by George J. Dyke of the *Times* until one day the irony of it struck her: "He gets paid for those reviews but, what is more important, he also gets free tickets to the concerts"! From that day she set her sights on Dyke's job. Since he was hale and hearty and showing no signs of retiring she knew her aspirations were not going to be realized immediately. So in 1939, using her father's banking connections, she took her first full-time job at the old Royal Bank on Government Street. She never severed her connection with the *Times*, however, but continued to write book reviews and the occasional concert review if Dyke was unavailable — all at two cents a word.

---

[2] Some of the biographical information used here has been abstracted from the Eulogy read by Dr. Reginald Roy at Audrey's funeral on 18 August 1993, and other data have been obtained from the second edition of the *Encyclopedia of Music in Canada* (Toronto, 1992, p. 661) and from her husband.

In 1941 Audrey met her future husband Maurice Johnson of Metchosin who was then involved in a rubber plantation in Malaya but home on leave. They were married before his return to Malaya but three months later the Japanese attacked. He was fortunate to escape back to Canada via Singapore. Meanwhile Audrey, disenchanted with her banking career, decided to do her part and joined the Canadian Women's Army Corps. Maurice was later to be commissioned in the Canadian Intelligence Corps, largely due to his fluency in Japanese. He ultimately went back to the Far East and did not return to Victoria until 1947.

Audrey's military career was short, for in 1944 she joined the *Times* staff as a columnist while continuing to write reviews on a per-word basis, and in 1947 she became a full-time member of the *Times* staff using the by-line "Audrey St. Denys Johnson" — the "St. Denys" in affection for her father whose name (Sidney) is an English corruption of the French St. Denys. If she was going to write about the arts she knew she had to know more than one who just occupies a seat in the auditorium. Since any attempt at higher education was cut short by the death of her father she knew if she were going to pursue her dream it would have to be by sheer will and whatever luck came her way.

She soon associated herself with the Victoria Theatre Guild in order to gain an inside knowledge of theatre. She made it her business to get to know Major Llewellyn W. "Bill" Bullock-Webster who was "Mr. Theatre" in Victoria in the 1930s and she later became a provincial drama adjudicator. Since summers were always a "slack time" for arts reporters she spent a summer studying theatre with Lister Sinclair at the Banff School of Fine Arts and another studying with Dorothy Somerset, Sydney Risk, and others at UBC. Other summers were spent attending arts events in other parts of Canada (including Stratford and Montreal) and the US in order to get a broader perspective than her isolated island life had formerly provided. It was not until she had become a seasoned reporter, however, that she gained a British perspective.

As Adele Lewis put it: "She did it all. She covered dance, theatre, the gamut of the Victoria Music Festival from speech arts, strings, woodwinds, piano, and voice to choir, band, and honours performances. She covered Symphony performances and the Victoria Operatic Society's productions of music theatre from Gilbert and Sullivan to *My Fair Lady*. She covered local recitals, the Art Gallery and private gallery showings, Langham Court, Bastion, Belfry, and ballet. The list is endless."

When she retired in 1987 her work on behalf of the arts in Victoria was recognized by many community groups. She was made a life member of the Victoria Symphony Society, the Greater Victoria Music Festival Association, the Victoria Theatre Guild, and the Victoria Conservatory of Music. She was made an Honorary Citizen of the City of Victoria and received a Certificate of Merit from the McPherson Foundation in addition to other citations.

As a journalist there were no shades of grey about Audrey — everything was black or white. This, for an arts journalist, is as it should be. Arts journalists who cannot take a stand — who cannot become impassioned about a subject — had better take on another career. You either loved Audrey as a journalist or you did not — there was no half measure. Again, this is the world the arts journalists adopt and they must, early on, resign themselves to the fact that "you cannot please all of the people all of the time" but, to quote her husband, "she had a good swing at it." But one thing is clear — she loved the arts and she knew how they could enhance the life of a community. She did everything in her power for more than fifty years to see that they survived and prospered in Victoria.

She was a little like a Jack Russell terrier in that when she got hold of some wrong that needed righting she simply refused to let go. A good example is the orchestra pit at the McPherson Playhouse. She started complaining about the size and depth of the pit when the McPherson was renovated in 1962 and she was still writing about its inadequacies when she retired 25 years later. While nothing has yet been done about the McPherson orchestra pit, she was more successful in other crusades. Another example of her tenacity was the seeming indifference of various city councils in financially supporting the arts to the level which she thought they justified.

There are at least 20 years of opinions on this subject in her files and some notable success stories. A particular gripe was the fact that the McPherson Playhouse did not give preferential rates to local arts organizations. Perhaps, in honour of Audrey, the city might now seriously consider both of these wrongs that need righting — but there, I have spent so much time with Audrey over the past several months that I am now beginning to sound like her.

In editing the original manuscript I have tried to remain as true to Audrey as I could while reorganizing certain material and correcting errors of fact where her normally infallible memory (true!) was certainly in error. The manuscript came to me in three large computer files. From the sub-headings included it appeared that each large file was eventually to become several smaller chapters so I reorganized the original material into the 18 chapters presented here, each dealing with a fairly discrete body of information. The Epilogue is drawn from several parts of the original manuscript.

In certain instances material from my files and information from others has been interpolated at the beginning or within certain chapters in order to provide necessary background. The endings of some sections and chapters have been re-written in order to provide a smoother transition to a subject which might formerly have appeared dozens of pages earlier (or later) in the original manuscript.

I trust that Audrey would be pleased.

R. Dale McIntosh
University of Victoria
November 1994

Acknowledgements

Several individuals have contributed to the editing of this manuscript. While I have a good knowledge of the facts with respect to musical developments in this city over the past 150 years, my knowledge of the other arts is less firm. I must first thank Maurice Johnson for patiently answering my many questions about specific parts of the manuscript that I did not understand or that troubled me for some reason. The wine was especially good!

Drs. Gwladys Downes and Colin Graham were both more than happy to review events with respect to the Art Gallery of Greater Victoria so that no error might creep into this section. The section on theatre in Victoria was read by Dr. John Gilliland and I thank him for the many excellent suggestions he made for improving it. I am further indebted to Professor John Krich and Dr. Harvey Miller for their constructive criticisms on the chapter related to the Phoenix Theatre of the University of Victoria and, in particular, that material related to the "Victoria Fair" incidents.

The chapter on Pacific Opera Victoria was read and emended for errors in fact by Adele Lewis, Erika Kurth, and Petta MacKenzie.

Most of the photographs were kindly supplied by the Victoria *Times-Colonist*. I wish to thank the photographers involved and the editor, John Wells, for permission to reproduce them here. I am also indebted to Doreen Ash who located much of the visual material in the *Times-Colonist*'s extensive files, to Ian McKain, who identified the provenance of several of the illustrations, and to Dierdre, who found the lost portrait.

For proofreading the manuscript in its several stages the editor is indebted to Drs. Gwladys Downes and Betty Hanley. Ted Wagstaff proofed the manuscript for inconsistencies and design faults in addition to errors in construction. This work was much improved through the application of his very considerable skills. The contributions of Guy Chadsey in helping to re-organize the work should also be acknowledged.

I also wish to thank Dr. Beverly Timmons for the title and Dr. Mavor Moore for his inspiring Foreword.

Part I

A Road Taken

CHAPTER ONE

City of Dreams

IT was a young city established on the southern tip of Vancouver Island, sired by the Hudson's Bay Company at the confluence of Georgia Strait and the Strait of Juan da Fuca. Named for a reigning Queen, it was chosen in its early youth to be the capital city of what was to be Canada's most westerly province.

It was a city that bore an air of nonchalance — that provided time and space for musing. It was complacent in its isolation and unconcerned that the rest of Canada considered it "quaint." It was dominantly populated by the descendents of pioneers from the British Isles and permeated by their view of life and the proper order of events. Here live-in maids, nannies, cooks, and even chauffeurs were not exceptional, murders (along with hurricanes) "hardly ever happened," and average householders seldom bothered to lock their houses when they went out to shop or visit. In fact it was so relatively crime-free that the police force was stirred up only when routine raids were undertaken on the generally innocuous Chinese gaming houses and opium-smoking dens on lower Fisgard Street or when the whorehouses spotted about in an adjacent area became too shamelessly obvious. At intervals it was deemed advisable to nudge the populace into an awareness of a police presence; replete with London-style Bobby helmets and carrying truncheons — no guns of course — they would magically appear.

The city of Victoria was so laid back in the early decades of the twentieth century that its citizens accepted with satisfaction and pride their isolation from the bustling mainland communities. It regarded the future warily and in a spirit of total conservatism.

Victoria was asserted by other Canadian cities to be so dated as to be, indeed, a pause in time — what might later be recalled as a sort of west-coast Brigadoon. It was a sleepy city that rolled up its sidewalks at nine of the clock each night, according to eastern visitors, and preserved an enveloping hush on Sundays when the principal downtown department store solemnly closed its curtains on all street display windows. This was where theatres — except movie houses and other performance places — mostly locked their doors and took a three-month vacation in the summers.

It was also a city where elderly trees were not only profoundly respected but had right-of-way and when municipalities established roads, traffic had to be routed around them. Fondly remembered by long-time Victorians, especially those living behind the "tweed curtain" in Oak Bay, was the towering old oak tree that reigned supreme through my younger years dividing St. David Street at midblock into south- and north-bound routes.

Victoria was a city that provided poets, artists, and children with space in which to breathe and dream over their imaginings; to acquire an affinity with the luxurious natural world that existed a few footfalls from their doorsteps. It permitted them to delude themselves into believing it was a world that would always be there — a world of wide, lush, and murmurous suburban areas where undisturbed woodlands sheltered delicate orchids, and the snowy splendour of triliums and Easter lilies in the spring. This was where upland fields were a living glaze of cerulean blue when the native camas was in flower; where skylarks soared filling the ocean-borne air currents with melody, and where in most suburban neighbourhoods there was space for privacy and clean sea air to breathe. Pheasant and quail uttered their mating calls at sunrise, and the dark hours were softly alive with the sound of night creatures. Thus it was to remain for many years of slow, inevitable, often stubbornly resisted change.

It was originally, in effect, a company town. The Hudson's Bay Company founded and nurtured it and it was, for a time, overseen by a Royal Navy presence. The population was a mixture of British colonists, artisans, and officials; aboriginal peoples; and Asians. Many families came from Great Britain to fill official posts — engineers, architects, law makers and interpreters, doctors, bankers, men of the cloth, as well as adventurers of many kinds and races.

Fine homes were soon established, many settlers bringing to this pioneer setting their families, ideals, and artifacts and treasures from the old lands. The fort also became a focus for those seeking a fortune in gold on three separate occasions: Barkerville in 1862, Leechtown (in the vicinity of Sooke) in 1864, and the Yukon in 1898. The population soon swelled and new professional and skilled tradesmen came from the British Isles to fill official and specialist jobs. Growth continued from settlement and fort into a town, then a city, and finally the provincial capital.

The identities of first families are reflected in the names of suburban areas such as Langford and Colwood, and in street names as such as Helmcken, Yates, Douglas, Blanshard, Pemberton, Trutch, and Menzies. Indigenous peoples are commemorated with road and area titles — Camosun, Saanich, Esquimalt, Songhees, Sassenos, Malahat, and Metchosin. From among first-settler families came those who would sow the seeds of foreign cultures to accompany the vital plantings of basic business and industry. Among them were photographers, woodworkers, painters, poets, scribes, musicians, and performers of all kinds and capabilities. Many of these latter were hobbyists who eased the homesickness and the hard facts of living in a pioneering community through artistic endeavours.

There was a minority among the new and growing population, especially those of a musical or theatrical persuasion, who could not conceive of a town or a city, of whatever size, existing without the arts. This left a majority who regarded the arts as a non-productive pastime — an occupation limited to those who had leisure to indulge in ordinarily unprofitable activity. This attitude was to persist in one way or another throughout the following several decades, only beginning to change noticeably in the years bracketed by the two world wars.

From the old countries there were, nevertheless, those who brought their parlour organs, their fiddles, and their pianos. The first piano on Vancouver Island came via clipper ship around Cape

Horn in 1853 and was said to be transported by Indians in a straw-lined cart from the Hudson Bay wharf to the new home of its owner, Mrs. Edward Edwards Langford who lived in that suburban area which now bears the family name. Tin trunks stuffed with music made the long journey around the Horn, including operetta scores by composers now long forgotten and considerable amounts of choral music. That most natural and flexible of all musical instruments, the human voice, was among the first cultured sounds of the old world to be heard on this otherwise richly endowed continental edge.

Anglican Bishop Edward Cridge brought his father's violoncello from Devonshire and often joined in on whatever cultivated music making there might be. Augustus Pemberton brought his flute and surveyor Benjamin W. Pearse his violin. This enthusiastic music making, if blithely amateur, was a notable improvement over Christmas at the fort in 1852 when no musical instrument whatever, not even a church bell, was available for celebration.

With the arrival of those who were to become the first citizens of Victoria came many heritage furnishings, paintings, bronzes, and noteworthy works of art in various media. These eclectic family treasures, brought to make the wilderness seem less untamed and the living more redolent of home, were harbingers of what this new-born city was to become.

Governor James Douglas, foreseeing the economic advantage to Fort Victoria in the goldrush years, declared it a free port in 1862. Despite a few substantial homes being built it was still, over large areas, something of a shack town. In the latter part of the 1860s, the goldrush booms having subsided, leading citizens were anxious to solidify the status of the island town and sought for it union with the mainland colony of British Columbia. This was somewhat grudgingly agreed to on 25 May 1868 and Vancouver's Island joined Confederation in 1871.

By Order-in-Council from Westminster, with considerable urging from Douglas and despite vociferous and bitter complaints from the mainlanders, Victoria was proclaimed the seat of government and the capital city of the united colonies of Vancouver's Island and British Columbia.

One of the first to promote the arts as a worthy activity for this new furthest-west capital was the so-called "hanging judge," Sir Matthew Baillie Begbie. Harsh as he may well have been on crooks and evildoers, he was friendly towards all the arts. Sir Matthew's particular interests were music and theatre. He was the instigator and first president of the Victoria Philharmonic Society in 1859. He purchased and transformed an abandoned Hudson's Bay Company fur warehouse on Government Street near Bastion Square into the city's first theatre. Named the Victoria Theatre, this 500-seat house was to host some notable performers, including the renowned nineteenth-century husband-and-wife team, Mr. and Mrs. Charles Keen. In deference to the namesake of the city, Begbie later added "Royal" to the name of his theatre.

Begbie also encouraged amateur theatrical performances, and his Philharmonic Society's instrumentalists provided the city's first orchestral accompaniment for musical productions. A suave and elegant figure, dramatic with his Van Dyke beard and flowing cape, he was a man of considerable humanity. Begbie was first among a series of personalities whose conviction, passion, perception, and expertise were to influence the remarkable cultural and artistic development of Victoria throughout the later nineteenth and twentieth centuries.

Over the latter half of the nineteenth century and into the twentieth there slowly emerged the beginnings of a cultivated and enriched society. Banks and churches, administrative offices, and important residences displayed the talents and inspiration of gifted architects such as Francis Rattenbury, Leonard James, and Samuel McClure, among others.

Growth continued into the first half of the new century, flourishing and producing some rare talents at an amateur level, falling, however, well behind the rapid development in Vancouver with its unarguable mainland advantage. A strong and arts-friendly business presence was a factor in encouraging and sustaining professional cultural activity. As time went on manufacturers on the island found the cost of shipping products to the mainland to be a serious disadvantage, eventually causing such important industries as Bapco Paint, the Silver Spring Brewery, and Sidney Roofing to leave the city in the years immediately following the Second World War. The serious promoters of fine arts development in British Columbia's capital saw them go with apprehension.

The degree of isolation from continental Canada by the eighty miles of straits water was regarded by some to be a distinct advantage. There were those among the new Canadians who saw the gradual melding of outlying communities on the mainland into the increasing sprawl of Vancouver as a threat, and relished the concept of Victoria being a separate and unique entity.

The city and its surroundings, indeed the entire southern area of Vancouver Island, proved to have a particular attraction for those newcomers who disliked the political climate of change in Britain, Asia, and the Far East where they had spent many years in the military, as civil service administrators, or in business. They were seeking a society that did not change, where the old values of the Edwardian era prevailed. For a time they found it and contributed to it largely in Victoria, Duncan, and adjacent communities. Their world was dominant in the south-island towns and outlying areas for more than twenty years before the mould began to crack as the patriarchs died off and World War II fought its way to a new era.

CHAPTER TWO

Early Experiences in the Arts

P IANO instruction had begun for me in Winnipeg at the age of five. Shortly after we became settled in Victoria, mother began to worry about my musical education, which she deemed as essential.

Enquiries through some contacts with musical organizations elicited the information that, aside from one or two individual teachers who did not accept beginners, there were two schools of music: the Columbia School of Music (which was downtown, situated in the building at the corner of Fort and Broad streets) and the Dominion Academy of Music. The latter sat atop the old Royal Bank building (long since replaced by a modern version) at the corner of Fort and Cook. This was mother's choice on the basis of it being "out of the busy business centre." Consultation with acquaintances indicated that the Dominion Academy had a reputation for getting most candidates through the Royal Schools examinations every year. A few weeks short of my eighth birthday, therefore, I was enrolled under the tutelage of the Academy's principal, "Madam" Kate Webb and her singular assistant, Miss Nellie Ella Mylam.

Madam was a stout lady and, when I first knew her, probably in her middle sixties. She wore pince-nez with a black cord anchored to her ample bosom. Her head, throughout the seven years of our acquaintance, was surmounted by a large brown doughnut of a transformation imprisoned in a fine net. She taught piano and singing and was pleasant enough to be remembered without rancour.

In striking contrast, Nellie Ella was the thinnest, flattest woman I have ever seen. Her shape might have been the inspiration for those old-style unsprung wooden clothespins. Even the back of her

9

head was flat and her straight dark hair, cut short at the nape, was plastered down with some sort of pomade. Occasionally some strands at the back detached themselves and stood away from her head like semaphore signals. Her finest feature was a pair of dark eyes set in a sallow face.

She undoubtedly was the brains and the shrewd business half of a partnership that had begun in England long before I knew them. Without Miss Mylam's talent for thrift and coiled-spring energy she and Madam Kate would never have been in a position to retire comfortably when the examining teams from London became younger and brought less forbearing attitudes to their work. Webb and Mylam, after some 20 years in Canada, returned to Britain with a decent nestegg of savings and bearing armloads of silverware nudged from presumably grateful parents by Nellie Ella.

Miss Mylam, besides teaching every day but Sunday, found time to keep the accounts, shop for their necessities and — as this 1920s odd couple lived on the premises behind closed doors that had once been offices — cook all the meals on a small gas stove in a one-time washroom-janitor's cupboard space. On Sundays she did the laundry and draped it around the big studio to dry. In addition, Nellie Ella made her own clothes. All her dresses were cut out of a cheap common fabric known as cotton crêpe. They were designed kimono-style with sleeves and body all in one, seamed up, machine hemmed, and girdled with a plain black belt.

On Saturdays Nellie Ella would wait until close to five o'clock before going out to buy their Sunday dinner. Her goal was the public market, located then on Fisgard in the area behind City Hall. Timing her arrival to coincide with the stall holders packing away their unsold goods she would be able to pick up a cut-price bird or bunny, most stall holders preferring to slash their price rather than cart the carcass home in the days before electric refrigeration. Otherwise, she confided once to my mother, they dined on a couple of eggs.

Madam Webb taught intermediate and senior piano, singing, and harmony. She would also take primaries like me if the parents

10

were willing to pay the top fee which was in the neighbourhood of seven dollars a month. Miss Mylam taught theory and beginner piano. Neither of them were better than mediocre teachers of musical performance. Nellie Ella, however, was first class in preparing students in theory and rudiments for music exams. She could read music though she had difficulty translating written music to the keyboard, as some of the senior students later discovered. The whole operation was something of a scam, dedicated solely to cramming hordes of students through the Royal Schools of Music exams year after year. The lists of successes were proudly displayed each year in the city's two dailies.

This pair generally represent what were acceptable music teaching standards in Victoria of the early and mid-twenties. All of this was to change and the city's standards of piano teaching and performance were soon to become considerably enriched, and were to remain so.

Near the end of my seventh year with Kate Webb, having glided through all the theory and rudiments for music exams with high marks and reached the advanced level of piano performance with nothing better than what I considered to be average results, I was becoming bored. The music put before me for study consisted mostly of Grieg and Cécile Chaminade and other even less arresting composers. No Schumann, Mozart, Beethoven, Bach, or even Mendelssohn.

Webb and Mylam soon observed a distinct downward trend in their exam results as younger, more searching and ruthless examiners replaced the old, and so the two announced their retirement. Taking over the school would be a professor and performer of piano from London's Royal Academy of Music named Stanley Shale.

On a soft November day in 1928 Stanley Shale arrived in Victoria. He was slight of build, handsome, shy with a distinctively English reserve, and totally dedicated to the art of piano performance and to teaching. He was, nevertheless, a visionary man but had one addiction — the movies. He came bearing a history of distinction and scholarship gained in the intense musical atmosphere of the Royal Academy where he had been a favourite student of Tobias Matthay, one of the era's most renowned and innovative of piano pedagogues. His teaching post at the Royal Academy had been interrupted by an agonizing neuralgia, the apparent result of his wartime experiences in London. The long-term effects of this were apparent even a decade later.

He had first heard of Victoria from his friend and fellow student Felix Swinstead, who had been one of the new wave of examiners who visited the wide-flung British dominions and colonies. Swinstead was, like Shale, a Matthay student as well as being a teacher at the Academy and a composer. Having just returned from a cross-Canada examining tour and finding his friend depressed, Swinstead told Shale about the beauty of Vancouver Island, the easygoing life of the province's capital, and especially about the Dominion Academy of Music with its more than 300 students in search of proper instruction. "There's a lot of talent there but the teaching standard is shocking," he told Shale. "It would be just the ideal situation for you — a healthy challenge."

On Shale's arrival there was a great bustle, a boiling of curiosity, and some apprehension. Certain fathers (including mine) thought a woman, no matter what her artistic status, was a more suitable teacher of music to their daughters. Stanley was officially welcomed by Madam Webb with a dress-up evening student recital. This was endured by Shale because, fortunately, he did possess an appreciation of the involuntary absurd. Much later he confided to me that he was appalled, not only with the standard of performance, but at the old-fashioned "dame school" presentation of students at the keyboard with Madam seated beside them — "as though she were prepared to rap their knuckles if they played a wrong note!" Nevertheless, he discerned the presence of some promising talent among those who had been selected to play.

Having completed all my written work by age 15, I was looking three years up the road to a teaching licentiateship. As part of the preparation I had become an aide to Nellie Ella by spending a couple of Saturday morning hours correcting beginners' theory books. It was on one of those Saturdays, Madam and Nellie Ella having departed for England only days before, that my entire concept of music, my life in fact, began to change.

Footsteps up the stairs and along the corridor heralded Professor Shale returning from a walk in the rain. He propped his open wet umbrella on the floor, flung his mackintosh across a chair and, massaging his hands, walked across to the shrouded Nordheimer grand piano accustomed to use only on state occasions. The shroud was swept off, the lid raised, and he began to play. I think it was something by Schumann, one of his favourite composers; then Chopin and a Beethoven Sonata movement; then Debussy. He played on with an occasional nod or murmured comment in my direction. I sat glued to my chair, hands tightly clasped, unable to move or utter a sound for fear the magic aura would be shattered. I know that from being a bored student and a willing though uninspired listener, I came in that one hour to a clear recognition of the power of music; to becoming an ardent student eager to commit many hours a day to the piano practise I had previously approached only half-heartedly.

Because of his nervousness — the after-effect of his neuralgia — Shale only played one public concert in Victoria. Those of us who frequented the studio, however, were often blessed with such impromptu recitals and they remain a lasting memory.

To say that Stanley Shale was a prime mover in raising and establishing a high standard of musical performance and teaching in Victoria is not to slight others who were important contributors. Notable in this capacity and a significant presence in the city prior to Shale's coming and after, was Gertrude Huntly Green. A fine Canadian pianist with an international reputation and a charming personality, she undertook solo engagements in the United States and Canada as well as abroad. For a number of years concert performance took precedence over teaching and consequently she accepted only a limited number of advanced students who worked with her when she was in the city.

The lasting importance of Stanley Shale's presence was the consistency with which he developed students over the period of nearly 25 years of his residence here. He inspired not only exceptional performers but highly gifted and qualified teachers. In doing so he created a teaching dynasty within this city and the province. Perhaps the most conspicuous example is Dr. Robin Wood, principal emeritus of the Victoria Conservatory of Music and Lansdowne Professor (retired) with the University of Victoria's School of Music. He, in turn, has produced some excellent teachers and performers, among them Jocelyn Abbott, Walter Prossnitz, May-Ling Kwok, and Robert Holliston. There are, in addition, a great many others now pursuing satisfactory national and international careers in both performing and teaching. Thus the dynasty founded by Stanley Shale has continued to the present third generation.

—◆—

When I was a pre-teenager only one magazine came regularly into our house, the *Saturday Evening Post*. It was read virtually cover-to-cover by my mother and grandmother who, despite their English classic education, relished the early Damon Runyon and Tugboat Annie stories as well as many others that were totally alien to their own language and experience. As for me, as soon as I could get my hands on an issue, I'd pore over the cover drawings and story illustrations, particularly those of Albert Payson Terhune (whose realist style was almost photographic) and, in contrast, Will Griffe (whose drawings were, I came to realize later, the better of the two, being less painstakingly photographic, more expressive and lively). Their influence on me was so profound that for a long while I promised myself that I would become an illustrator for the *Post* when I grew up.

As I grew into my mid-teens, however, with music the central object of my life, the art school dream faded as also did the presence of artist-illustrators in magazines. I came, in my final year of music exams and student teaching, to the realization that I had no desire to perform publicly, nor did I relish the idea of a lifetime of teaching youngsters whose interests in piano were largely parent-imposed.

It was while I was attempting to deal with these inner conflicts that I met Ina Uhthoff, herself a fine artist and a dedicated teacher. I showed her some drawings and sketches and asked her if she considered that I had enough talent to enrol in her art school. She replied that she closed her school in the spring but that she would be teaching at the six-week-long Provincial Summer School for teachers who wished to upgrade or add to their skills. She suggested that I should register and attend her classes.

I followed her advice, found it an exhilarating experience, and in the fall entered her school as a full-time student. I was able to attend life classes; learn pastel and charcoal techniques; and become involved in the designing, carving, and printing of wood and lino blocks. I never got as far as watercolour, gouache, oil, or mixed media as I was forced to leave before the year ended. My father had become fatally ill and I was needed at home to help cope with the nursing.

After he died I did two things that were to affect all the rest of my life: I became a member of the Canadian Authors' Association (CAA) and joined the Victoria Little Theatre. Both were good decisions. The CAA lead me directly to the doorstep of my lifetime career and the Little Theatre to a recreational activity that I found deeply rewarding.

Through at least a decade and a half of growing up, my mother's passion for music and theatre of all kinds meant we never missed attending when a touring company or a musical luminary came to the Royal Victoria Theatre. During the winter season in those days they came regularly. I remember attending concerts by such legendary artists as pianists Paderewski, Josef Hoffman, Percy Grainger, and Vlademir de Pachmann; singers Dame Clara Butt,

Amelita Galli-Curci (long after she should have retired), John McCormack, Tito Schipa, and superb contralto Ernestine Schumann-Heink; and violinists Fritz Kreisler, Mischa Elman, and Efrem Zimbalist, among others.

I developed a taste for theatre as well through excursions to see the British Shavian Players doing a Shaw repertoire and the Sir Barry Jackson Company. The company presented in Victoria a repertory that included works by James Barrie, Bernard Shaw, and Oliver Goldsmith. Playing major roles in this company was Donald Wolfit, one of the most distinguished West End actors of his era, who later formed his own Shakespeare company which he brought across Canada to the west coast on at least two occasions. His Malvolio in *Twelfth Night* was the most memorable I have seen among several fine productions including the Stratford (Ontario) Festival of 1953. Wolfit was also notable for his interpretation of King Lear and this, too, he brought to Victoria.

In addition to these there were the visits, on at least three occasions, of London's D'Oyly Carte Opera Company performing a repertoire of authentic Gilbert and Sullivan, richly mounted and featuring the celebrated London cast. The English Carl Rosa Opera came quite regularly to offer performances of some of the most popular Italian grand operas including *Pagliacci, Cavalleria Rusticana, La Traviata, Il Trovatore, Madama Butterfly*, and even *Aida*. To top it all off the Ballet Russe de Monte Carlo was virtually an annual visitor to the Royal, bringing such stars as Alexandra Danilova partnered by Frederic Franklin, and others who were to become living legends.

The local scene was not entirely barren in the early thirties. A small number of professional or professionally-directed productions occurred on the home front. The most popular among these being the Reginald Hincks Company doing what he described as "potted operas" in a small legitimate theatre on Yates Street east of Blanshard known as the Playhouse. Later revamped for cinema, this theatre became the Haida. To the best of my recollection we seldom missed any of their presentations.

16

The accent of this company was on broad comedy, partly because of the popularity of their ace comedian-character actor, Ernie Petch. A natural clown and inevitable scene-stealer, he was a member of a gifted Victoria family. Another feature of every show was a couple of good songs, arbitrarily inserted by Hincks in the script whether they belonged there or not, to display the talents and lovely cultivated soprano of their leading lady, auburn-haired Eva Hart.

The company eventually fell apart following the suicide of their leading man and other problems. Eva, however, continued to reign as Victoria's leading soprano for some time, until finally she retired from the concert stage after her marriage to Col. J. Q. Gillan. As for Hincks, he maintained a strong presence in the city's theatrical scene for some years, frequently being called on to bring his expertise to the direction of the annual Christmas pantomimes.

My first practical experience with the theatre on a large scale was when, at the age of 11, I met Bill Bullock-Webster — popularly known as the "Major." A notice had been published in the press regarding a pageant to be staged in the horse show building situated in the fairgrounds in the Oak Bay Willows area. Among the classic stories I knew so well by heart from my mother's tellings and my own perusals, was Scott's *Ivanhoe*. I loved that romantic tale and when I read that the great jousting scene was to be enacted — complete with horses bearing knights in armour fighting for the hand of the beautiful Rowena, the whole scene to include hordes of villagers and lords and ladies — I became most interested. When I found, furthermore, that those interested in participating should attend a casting, I gave mother no peace until she agreed, cautiously, to let me attend. The day was won through pointing out that my reddish-blonde pigtails made me a perfect example of a Saxon child.

The pageant was staged, complete with aristocrats in velvet and ermine, satins and jewels, a lovely Rowena and a sorrowful Rachael, and among the peasantry a gaggle of children, one of whom had ginger-blonde braids. All of us youngsters watched with genuine excitement as knights (featuring the Major) mounted on horses from the Carley stables (and including Carley himself) galloped up and down the sawdust with levelled lances. It was my first on-stage appearance in a drama, excluding those I used to invent for my playmates in which I starred myself and which were based on stories I had read.

At that point in my life I abandoned an artist's career and seemed destined for the stage. Our neighbours had a girl a little older than I, and a son a little younger. Unknown to me they had been building a stage in their basement, all equipped with draw curtain and lights. When it was finished they came to my mother, who was known for her writing skill and love of theatre, and asked her if she could create a drama for them out of the story of Bluebeard. She provided them with a script and the next problem was to cast it.

Up to this point I had nothing to do with the project but it seemed that Jessie's best friend was too shy to play the heroine, Fatima. So I was invited in and mother was again consulted and provided costumes. Tickets had been sold to neighbours for a nickel each and we were assured a good house. Only one thing went wrong. Jessie had claimed the title role for herself without realizing that, except for the opening scene, Bluebeard would be off-stage for almost the entire play while Fatima, daintily veiled and silken-clad with flowing locks, would be on stage throughout with her calls of "Sister Ann, Sister Ann, do you see anyone coming?"

To make things worse, at a lemonade-and-cookies theatre party upstairs Jessie's father kept enthusiastically referring to me as "the neighbourhood's own Mary Pickford!" It was my first time on stage and the first and last time I ever upstaged anybody.

Having been mesmerized by what I had seen and participated in on the stage, I joined the Little Theatre in 1933. Within a few months I was totally absorbed. Nothing in my previous experience had so engrossed me. To be actively engaged in the making of theatre was, it appeared, a manifold experience calling on all one's creative ability. I began my theatre career by working backstage, where I laboured at chores such as prompting, and assisting with sets, props, and costumes. From this vantage point I was able to view the whole process of creating theatre. I observed that most

18

amateur directors approached what should have been the highly-creative task of interpreting a playscript by simply copying, in detail, movement and action as prescribed in the script, stage directions which had been copied from notes taken at rehearsals for the original production. There must be, I thought, something more creative to the directing of a play than an obsequious, to-the-letter following of a previous director's work. It was at that point that I determined to learn all I could about the process of directing, but other challenges were to intervene before I was to pursue this opportunity.

CHAPTER THREE

Getting from A to B with No Easy Lessons

IT was a fall evening in 1933 when Fate first crooked a beckoning finger in my direction. Professor Shale, with whom I had studied piano and harmony for the past six years had given me a ticket to a piano recital by visiting American pianist-composer, Charles Wakefield Cadman.

Standing near the entrance to the Empress Hotel Ballroom I was waiting for a friend to join me. In those years performers of world status were presented at the Royal Victoria, but most recitals and small-group concerts took place in the Empress Hotel Ballroom, there being no suitable alternative venue outside church halls and high school auditoria which are notoriously lacking in acoustical as well as posterior comfort.

My eye lighted on an elderly man talking to a group of people who seemed to hang on his words as he stabbed at the programme with his finger. I recognized him as the Victoria *Daily Times* music critic, George J. Dyke. I was close behind him as we entered the ballroom and observed that he merely nodded to the ticket taker without surrendering a ticket. Then it actually struck me for the first time — he attends all these events free! And then came another revelation — he gets paid for what he writes as well!

"What a piece of cake," I thought enviously. The poverty of the average youth in those depression years was endemic, especially so among students of all kinds. When it came to music one really felt the squeeze. There was music to buy and the necessity to listen to quality recordings for serious students planning to teach. There were instruments to maintain, pianos to be tuned, strings replaced and bows rehaired, and reeds and other maintenance for wind players. As well there were lessons and exam fees, and a student also needed to hear as much live performance as possible. In the years since my generation little has changed except the soaring cost of services and supplies in keeping with the general economy.

The idea of free access to musical events and being paid for writing about them continued to obsess me. I had recently achieved a diploma in piano (which included theory and harmony) from the combined Royal Academy and Royal College of Music in London, England. That was a goal achieved over more than a decade of piano practice and study involving six to eight hours a day. Being awarded the highest mark in the province up to that time and being congratulated by the examiner on my interpretation of the French Impressionists were unexpected achievements that produced an inflated amount of self-confidence.

From that night of the Cadman recital I had my sights fixed, quite determinedly, on Mr. Dyke's job. I was brought up short when it occurred to me that Dyke would first have to retire. So I waited, hopeful but patient, hoping only that he should enjoy a happy retirement — soon!

One favourite occupation of my early childhood had been the inventing of stories carried out in a series of drawings in unruled exercise books. I daydreamed about becoming an illustrator of children's books like those that came from my English aunt and were illustrated by such geniuses as John Tenniel and, especially, Arthur Rackham and Kate Greenaway. Art, poetry, inventing stories — all these were my sources of happiness and satisfaction. I loved the creative aspect of the arts too much to settle, as my father thought I should, in the sole pursuit of performing and teaching music. I had come to know better than anyone that I did not possess the singular and absolute dedication of the successful teacher, the ability to create musically, or the physical structure and emotional balance required by the performer. Yet neither of my parents ever discussed with me the need to become a wage-earner.

There was a clear indication that an inherited talent for prose and, to a minor degree, poetry, was dominating several other interests of my late teens when I joined the Canadian Authors' Association. Some published poetry and the odd piece of prose encouraged my ambition. This was also to lead in a roundabout fashion to the realization of my music/journalist target and what was eventually to become my chosen career for over fifty years.

Before any writings of mine were published, however, my father died after a two-year battle with cancer that had forced him into early retirement. The Great Depression was still maintaining its grip and mother was left with sizeable hospital and medical bills, a small pension, and a large house surrounded by two-thirds of an acre of beautiful garden. Housing sales at the time, as well as prices, were at rock bottom. It was difficult enough keeping myself in hosiery, writing paper, and typewriter ribbons, let alone being able to afford tickets for the musical and dramatic events I yearned to attend. So I focused more consistently on George Dyke's reviews, learning a good deal in the process as to approach and style in the handling of commentary in matters musical. It also became apparent that George did not by any means cover everything. Many things went unmentioned in the press, particularly when dates clashed.

My first experience with newspaper writing, however, had nothing to do with music or, in its narrowest sense, the arts. The Canadian Authors' Association had initiated an annual Canadian Authors' Week and the local Victoria and Island Branch contributed by getting the editor of the *Times* to provide a Saturday page devoted entirely to reviews of Canadian authors' works published during the current year. As a member of the Association and one who had some poetry published in the annual chapbooks and elsewhere, I was asked to review a book of poems and submit it to the city editor, Mr. Archie Wills.

Invading the foreign territory with some apprehension and having been directed to the desk of Mr. Wills, I handed over my manuscript with confidence oozing out through my shoelaces. Mr. Wills skimmed the first couple of paragraphs then glanced through the rest of the review reading here and there. He looked at me thoughtfully.

"This will be fine," he said, dropping my manuscript into a tray on his desk. "You have quite a flair. How would you like to review some of the books we get from publishers from time to time?"

Little did Archie Wills know what he was getting into. I was three feet off the ground, hardly able to believe what I was hearing. Although a diet of reviewing books was what I had in mind, I knew a foot-in-the-door when I thought I saw it. His next words brought me down to earth with a thump.

"Of course we don't pay for the reviews but you can keep the books."

Since I was a dedicated member of the Public Library it was not books for which I was starved. I took a deep breath. Obviously it would be unwise to kill the goose that was about to lay even a brass egg at my feet. I thought of the alchemist who turned dross into gold. Yes, I would review some books, I told him, but "I'd rather review music events." I went on to provide him with my qualifications, emphasizing the fact that I had my Licentiate from the Royal Schools of Music in London. Mr. Wills said that was certainly impressive but added, however, that they already had a music reviewer. I offered him the argument that lots of events were not covered because one person couldn't be everywhere.

He admitted the point. "Well," he said, "if something comes up and George can't make it for one reason or another, we'll give you a try. In the meantime how about reviewing these." He handed me three books. Don't ask me what the subjects were — they were entirely forgettable.

Fortunately for me, "something" came up quite soon. Since I'm not a diarist nor an ardent record keeper by nature, I've no recollection of what the event was — something local, undoubtedly. The pay was two cents a word which, considering the required brevity of any piece covering the arts, was not going to render me a self-supporting wage earner. It was better, however, than teaching piano and theory at four dollars a month for a 45-minute weekly lesson (the going rate for undistinguished teachers at the time) and, in some cases, having to wait a couple of months to be paid.

Meanwhile the *Times* seemed to be satisfied with my contributions and an intermittent yet ongoing trickle of assignments came my way. Archie Wills was a good coach on the demands and style of newspaper commentary. He taught me the discipline of "cut and cut some more" even when you thought you'd pared the fat to the bone. He taught me to be on guard against the clichéd words and phrases that come, to misquote Shakespeare, "so trippingly to the fingertips." Archie didn't soft-shoe around with his criticisms. He made his point and drove it home. On the other hand if he liked something he said that too in the same spare language he used in his writing. He held to one maxim that I never forgot — the word "very" is the most unnecessary word in the English language. Archie was a journalism school in himself.

The day inevitably came when George J. Dyke, growing elderly, decided to retire and wrote his final "30."[1]

I held my breath, but in vain. The *Times* managing editor was not about to hand over the critic's desk to a young woman not yet 20. Instead he called on the Christ Church Cathedral organist and choir master, Stanley Bulley, to take over. I was assured I would still be asked to fill in the blanks. To this I resigned myself realizing, in spite of my cocksureness, that I could not compete with someone much older and more experienced than me. The pleasure derived from listening to more music than I could possibly afford and then writing about it somewhat compensated for disappointments and the meagre pay.

In the meantime I had made some friends among the regular denizens of the *Times* newsroom and the desire to become a genuine full-time colleague was thus based on more than a paycheque, though the latter continued to be an important factor. In desperation I completed a secretarial course but even typing, shorthand, and simple bookkeeping skills did not immediately provide me with an income. Neither did having friends in high places, one of these

---

1 In the now departed era of typed copy, the figure 30 was used to signify the end of an article.

being a deputy minister in the legislature and the father of a girl I knew well.

I made an appointment with him, not specifically seeking a civil service job, but more for advice on how to locate and approach a possible employer. He seemed uncomfortable and finally suggested that he had no idea what my politics were. I asked him if it made a difference if I joined a specific youth party, to which he replied that it would indeed. Having no interest whatever in politics I couldn't go that route. Instead I went to see the manager of the Royal Bank main office (now Munro's book store). Mr. Stevens had been a friend and associate of my father and was most anxious to help me. So my first employer turned out to be that branch of the Royal Bank of Canada.

The *Times* newsroom was still my favourite target, but patience, and almost everything I possessed, was wearing thin. Hopes were roused when Stanley Bulley, in the early years of the war, decided to move to Ontario. Bulley's departure was not followed, however, by an offer of full-time employment. Instead the by-line of a newcomer — a woman reporter from back east — began appearing regularly on the entertainment page. She was apparently a full-time newsroom staff member, something there seemed no possibility of my ever attaining.

The bank work turned out to be as much of a nightmare as I had imagined. Having been taken on as a junior secretary (due to the pressure of young men leaving to join the forces) I found myself before long having to deal every day with debit and credit handwritten entries in the current account ledgers — I whose handwriting pace would make a snail look brisk. It would have been embarrassing, but a relief, if they'd tossed me out after a trial run. But worse was to come when two more fresh-faced 18-year-olds left to join the airforce.

Then there fell to my lot a nightmare entitled "cash items." This daily chore consisted of floods of cheques drawn on other banks and masses of cashed-in stock coupons. All of these had to be listed in detail and balanced with the general ledger before I could stagger home to a late, late dinner. I was totally out of my depth and beginning to have frantic dreams about it.

One summer Saturday I came to the realization that, for sanity's sake, I had to find another job — though where and what I hadn't a clue. I was dead tired as well as depressed. The supposed half-day had, as was often the case, delayed us until almost four o'clock because of a general ledger error. Climbing into the Oak Bay bus, I found myself wishing I hadn't invited our longtime friend Ed Balsom to drop in for tea. The object was to cheer my mother up. Her recovery from 'flu was accompanied by sighs and lamentations over her loneliness and my long banking hours. I was dead tired, my nerves were frazzled, and I didn't feel like entertaining anyone — not even Ed, much as I enjoyed his intelligent conversation, love of music, and flattering attention whenever he entered the room.

As I walked up the drive that Saturday I saw that there was a strange car parked in the turnabout. As Ed didn't have a car I presumed someone else was visiting. I went into the kitchen and put the kettle on. Ed had heard the rattle of cups and came down the long hall to tell me who the visitor was, a longtime friend of his who had been away for four years in Malaya. "He's entertaining the mater with all sorts of stories. His name's Maurice Johnson. He's a pal of mine, home on five months' leave from managing a rubber plantation. You'll like him." I did and the liking was mutual. Ed and Maurice went off together after tea to visit other friends and then phoned me: if they came by to pick me up would I go with them on a pub crawl. I loathed beer but I said "yes." And I said "yes" again a few weeks later when Maurice proposed.

We were married in June and had two idyllic summer months together before he was off, back to the vital wartime production of rubber. I was expected to be joining him in the following spring but the gods of war had other plans for us.

Restless and lonely, I joined the Canadian Women's Army Corps (CWAC), went into training at Work Point Barracks, and was attached to the Royal Canadian Engineers because my art training had included a course in draughting. As Pearl Harbor went up in smoke the Japanese began their invasion down the Malay Peninsula and correspondence with Maurice was cut off except for an occasional three- or four-word cable. Following the fall of Singapore there was an anxious six-week period with no news. Finally word came from External Affairs and the Canadian Red Cross that Maurice had been ordered to accompany an official escape party out of Singapore just hours before it fell and had miraculously made it to the Australian port of Fremantle. From Perth he would be taking a ship home. It was a day I shall never forget. I was called to the telephone in the Engineers' draughting room from the CN telegraph office and the clerk's first words were "I have good news for you, Mrs. Johnson." The Engineers gave me the day off and told me to celebrate.

Maurice, debilitated by a variety of jungle-induced health problems, was home long enough to regain his normal fitness. He then applied and was accepted for Canadian army service and subsequently transferred to the Intelligence Corps following a crash course in spoken and written Japanese (he was already familiar with Tamil and Malay languages). Once again he was shipped off to South-East Asia.

Upon Maurice's return from the Singapore disaster I received a compassionate discharge from the CWAC. Leaving the army was not without its moment of regret for me as I'd been selected for officer training, which might have led to a possible posting overseas. With Maurice gone again and my *Times* connection on indefinite hold I felt like a useless piece of flotsam.

With more leisure time on my hands I once again became active with the Little Theatre. I needed permission to make a purchase for a stage production so dropped into the Bank of Montreal main office where the Little Theatre's treasurer was a member of the accountant's department. Surprisingly, he asked me if I was interested in a job and suggested I speak to the manager about joining their staff. I was astonished, remembering with not much fondness my earlier financial career. He stated that they were desperate; they would take anyone who had some banking experience

— even a woman — and even if she was wearing a gold band on her left fourth finger. "It wouldn't commit you to anything just to have a word with the manager," he said.

I had that word and the next day a phone call from the branch manager on the corner of Government and View streets. He would like to see me. I was not at all certain I wanted to see him but I nevertheless came out of his office with a job. It paid me almost twice what I had been earning during my previous bank encounter — the seemingly generous amount of $90 a month! This was viewed as a substantial salary at that time, especially for a woman. It was the beginning of a breakthrough for women that the war had created.

I pushed any idea of further journalistic activity into the background but a few days later found myself once more in the *Times* newsroom. Archie Wills had tracked me down at the bank — the first contact we'd had for several months. He wanted me to review an event taking place the next evening.

From the tone of his familiar voice I realized that he was somewhat stressed. So I skirmished. "I've got a full-time job now," I pointed out.

"Yes, but you're free at night."

"Some nights. I'm working in a bank!"

"Well, some nights, yes. But how about tomorrow?"

"I've sold my typewriter." (True: I was saving to buy a new one.)

"That's no problem. You can come up to the newsroom and write your review."

The will to resist was weakening. "What's happened to your regular reviewer? Has she had a breakdown?"

There was a slight pause. "You might say that. . ." Then dryly: "Did you read her review of *Blossom Time* in yesterday's edition?"

I had not. Archie told me to get a copy and read it. "When you've read it you'll know why she's no longer with us." I told him that being used as a convenience and then shunted aside for someone from another city or country was no longer acceptable to me. I launched into a critical review of my years of writing for the *Times*, pointing out that I had been told on several occasions that when so-and-so left I would become the regular reviewer.

"Look," he said, "if you want the job it's all yours from now on. Will you cover tomorrow night's event?"

What could I say. The opportunity I'd been aiming at for so long had suddenly dropped into my lap after I'd almost stopped dreaming about it. It felt just as good as I'd ever imagined. I found a copy of the *Times* and turned to the entertainment page. The touring company performing *Blossom Time* had originated in the United States and, according to word that went around, was mostly forgettable. Even so, the trampling it got from the reviewer could be likened to kicking a lame dog. There were several close-to-scurrilous comments on aspects of the chorus and the directing but what had brought the company manager to the point of seeing a lawyer and informing the *Times* of an imminent libel suit was the comment that one of the female principals had a voice obviously "forced down an octave by the ravages of time, gin and cigarettes." *Times* management — it was then owned by the Spencer family — were counselled to make an out-of-court settlement, which they did.

I was curious as to how this review had passed the city desk editors and got into print. I later discovered that it was not carelessness on their part, but wiliness induced by irritation on the part of the reviewer. She had been harbouring resentment over a typical small-town policy at the editorial desk of never saying anything that would hurt or embarrass a local performer — or even statements seemingly overtly discourteous to visiting artists. Determined to outwit the constant desk blue-pencilling of her work the critic, instead of leaving her copy in the editor's tray for morning perusal, as was the rule, took an unheard-of step. Upon finishing the piece she went directly to the composing room and handed it to the foreman of the night shift as ready copy. In doing so she achieved her aim but had written the obituary of her Victoria *Times* career. The moral here was clear to anyone taking over her desk: whatever you have to say be honest and firm in your opinions, but do not express them in terms that will land your newspaper in court with a libel suit.

I went back into reviewing, spending a couple of late nights a week, on average, at concerts and in the newsroom, but continued my 9 a.m. arrivals at my bank as a kind of insurance. One day Archie told me he would like to see me begin writing a weekly column. Uncharacteristically, I didn't leap at this opportunity. The prospect of being irrevocably committed to finding a subject and producing a column of several hundred words every week while coping with cash and balancing ledgers at the bank unnerved me. For the next few weeks Archie persisted and I resisted but in the end he won by simply saying he wanted a column in his hands within the next six days. He got it, of course.

The subject of that first column which appeared on 7 November 1947 was introduced with a question: "How many serious vocal students, I wonder, realize the importance of finding the ideal range for their voice?" The column attempted to point out the difference the appropriate range might make "between a successful career and mediocrity." It was illustrated with the story of the great Wagnerian tenor Lauritz Melchior's unimpressive operatic debut as a baritone singing Silvio in *I Pagliacci* at the Copenhagen Royal Opera. A perceptive American singer in the cast was sufficiently impressed by many aspects of his performance to tell Melchior his voice was wrongly placed. She urged him to sacrifice his repertoire and add several additional years of study to his life in order to develop his tenor range. "The fact that he accepted the advice was to give us, in the opinion of experts, the greatest heroic tenor since Jean de Reszke," said the column.

I've never found time to figure out how many hundreds of thousands of words rolled out of my typewriter, and later computer, to make up these columns. I only know for sure that many of them were a challenge and an inspiration — some as heady as champagne before breakfast and others a chore, churned out under pressure and not inspired in any sense. But I like to think that a reasonable number were possibly quite useful and sometimes intellectually challenging.

CHAPTER FOUR

New Directions and Responsibilities

A T the war's end the bank became a part of my past. At home I tackled creative writing again, including the writing of radio scripts. Two of these were accepted by the CBC and one, *The Cavendish Women*, was later aired. With my husband out of the army and seeking to establish a new career in the homeland he had left at age 20, I once more needed the stability that newspaper work offered. The summers continued to be arid in the entertainment department and it occurred to me that I need not necessarily stick to writing on music and theatre. I tackled the new managing editor, Leslie Fox. Archie Wills, having found various changes in policy by new owners conflicting with his own entrenched beliefs, had taken an early retirement. Ownership of the paper had also transferred from the Spencer family to Max Bell of Calgary. The new and memorable publisher was Stuart Keate and to my delight both Fox and Keate were greatly supportive of the arts.

I suggested to Les that there was no reason for me to stick exclusively to writing about the arts and proposed that I substitute for various reporters on holiday. He accepted this idea. This was a time when the city newspapers belonged to a local union. Later, when we became represented by the continent-wide American Newspaper Guild, freelancing was a hot issue and finally eliminated. A week or so later Fox phoned me and with his call my foot was on the second rung of the ladder to a permanent position. One of the two young assistants to women's page editor Elizabeth Forbes was going on holiday. Would I like to take her place for the next two weeks? I would.

I had known Elizabeth ("Bess") — an older woman than I — for some years. She had been a member of the advertising department staff but, like me, had persistently attempted to gain something more challenging. She was then head of the editorial third floor's social department. This enclave was virtually the paper's only acknowledgement of women's role at the vital core of the daily press. At the time I first set foot in the newsroom there was only one female reporter, Aileen Campbell. Attractive, intelligent, and extremely capable, Campbell later moved to Vancouver with her husband and became a top-line reporter for the Vancouver *Province.*

Although I intensely disliked the social department work, finding it snobbish and boring, I admired Bess in spite of this and also because she was a perfectionist. It was to her I later owed skills I was unlikely to have learned otherwise.

When an opportunity came for her to go to Japan for five weeks to do stories on the social problems of Japanese women, my first big chance came. Since I was older than the teenage girls who were usually her assistants and also had office experience I was called in, given a two-week crash course in women's page preparation and editing, and left in charge with an eighteen-year-old assistant. This was certainly stress I was not used to. The job started at 7 a.m. — I've never been a willing early riser — to get the page layouts to the composing room not a minute later than 9 a.m. Then it was on with the following day's stories, social notes, wedding descriptions in detail, cut-lines for pictures, then finally proofreading that day's page dummies when they came up from the composing room. In the back of your mind all this time lurked the thought that you had to come up with some special feature for the Saturday edition's section front page.

The rewards were that I was on regular salary for those five weeks but, most importantly, that I got to know the composing room and its crew. They remain in my memory as good-hearted and co-operative. This was to have a lasting impact through the years to come, for to understand how the entire structure that supports and carries forward your own particular strand makes you more efficient and the whole production smoother. Even so the production staff put up with a lot from me, including squeezing deadlines and occasionally seeking last-minute changes. However, no one ever fumed or swore at me — at least not in my presence.

The worst moment of my editing experience came on the last Saturday before Bess's return. We had planned a page of engagement pictures for the section front. On the dummy it looked fine but when the first press run circulated through the upstairs offices a breathless girl from advertising came upstairs to tell me that we had mis-mated two couples — one of the brides-to-be happening to be a friend of hers. Horror-stricken, I had to report the error to Les but again he and the compositors came up trumps. Nobody made a big issue out of it and the second press run was corrected.

When my tour of duty was finished and I thankfully handed over the office to Bess there was an unexpected bonus. Les told me he and Stu Keate did not think it fair that I should have to go back entirely to space rate pay so they proposed to pay me $40 a month for my columns in addition to space rates for my reviews. I was delighted that they were satisfied with my cruise on Bess's deck. The whole experience, however, was to lead me finally to my never forgotten goal.

Having acquired the know-how of editing and page layout I was able to spend a few hours each week helping one-time city editor Tom Merriman, a veteran whose First World War leg injury was beginning to trouble him greatly. A necessary but not too demanding niche had been arranged for Tom involving only the Saturday edition feature pages, which carried book reviews and building and garden features. By this time both the *Times* and *Colonist* were owned by Thomson Newspapers and had moved from their city centre location to share a new two-storey building on Douglas near Hillside. Circulation and business offices occupied the street-level floor while editorial offices, newsrooms, library, and composing room were on the upper level. The *Times* newsroom and editorial offices were situated at the south end and the *Colonist* had similar space at the north.

The only direct access to the editorial rooms was a fairly long flights of stairs, an uncomfortable walk for somebody with a disability. For Tom, whose injury was becoming worse with time, there were increasingly occasions when he could not make this journey at all. Most of the subjects he dealt with were familiar to me so I got into the habit of going into his tiny corner office, straightening up his desk, sorting the material for the coming weekend, and even writing a few cutlines and heads or a book review when deadlines were pressing.

When it was finally announced that Tom would not be coming back, city editor Lloyd Baker asked me if I could pinch-hit for a while with some of the newsroom fellows helping me out whenever they had time. There was no problem for me as to heads and cutlines thanks to what I had learned from Bess and Tom. Most of the weekend feature pages, aside from the garden column by Victoria experts Jack and Hilda Beastall and a syndicate feature on building, were largely filled with copy from the wire service. I knew I could step into Tom's shoes but I also knew now where the problem lay in assuming a dual role — arts editor and Tom's former work.

When I was speaking to Les one day I had referred to my long-nurtured desire to depart from freelancing and become part of the newsroom gang permanently. He replied: "We'd like that too but unfortunately your overtime (the amount of night work) would be too rich for our blood."

I told Les that Tom's work could be fit easily into my reviewing and column stint and, furthermore, that I would not demand overtime pay if I could substitute three or four days off a month in lieu.

He said, "You'd really be satisfied with that arrangement?"

"Of course," I told him, "I have a home and husband to look after. Those free days would be terrific."

"I think we have a deal," he said.

Two days later my long trek ended — I was no longer a freelancer. Thus I was able to become involved full-time in what would turn out to be Victoria's richest period of growth in the arts.

℘

Part II

Curtains Rising

CHAPTER FIVE

The Altar of St. Cecilia

I N its early decades Victoria was quite naturally a choral town. During that period when the settlement was simply a Hudson's Bay trading post, whatever music-making took place was in the form of song as there were no instruments available. Thus, much of the local music making at the time was choral and most of it was somewhat better than average. This was often confirmed by visiting musicians and, after 1927, by British festival adjudicators.

The first truly "professional" musicians to arrive in Victoria were choral conductors and organists who had gained appointments at local churches, and many choirs were developed under conductors who were basically well trained and, by nature, exceptionally gifted. Among the most outstanding of these which come to mind were Benedict Bantly, Gideon Hicks, George Jennings Burnett, Jackson Hanby, and Frederick Chubb. All these were known by name and musical reputation from the west coast to Toronto and other points east.

Among memorable conductors whose work was an influential factor in heightening the awareness, quality, and appreciation of music in BC's capital was Frank Tupman, who stood out not only for his leadership of the Victoria Male Voice Choir (a rival to the older Arion Club), but also for the high level of expertise he brought to the public schools' development in this medium. Another exceptional talent was Victoria-born Dudley Wickett who conducted The Meistersingers, an enjoyable and consistent festival prize-winning male ensemble, for a number of years.

A few made the church outstanding as a musical resource, enriched its services and, being experienced teachers, developed some fine solo voices. Roberto and Mary Wood, who came to Victoria from Winnipeg in 1949 to be music director and organist respectively of the First United Church, were among these.

Stanley Bulley, a personal friend of the British composer Gustav Holst, was brought from Britain in 1929 to establish the tradition of English cathedral music at Christ Church Cathedral. With his background and superior musical skills it was natural that Bulley should aspire to the production of some of the greatest of church music during his 15 years there. These included performances of Bach's *Christmas Oratorio* (1932), the Brahms *Requiem* (1932, 1936), and many performances of *Messiah*.

For such performances Bulley augmented the cathedral choir by the addition of experienced choral singers in the city, as well as bringing together orchestral musicians who had been the nucleus of several early attempts to create a permanent civic orchestra. This all led to the formation of the Choral and Orchestral Union which, just after Graham Steed's term in 1952, became the Victoria Choral Society. This development also gave encouragement to those instrumental performers whose determination was to see an orchestra take root and grow in what they persisted in viewing as fertile soil.

Graham Steed, later to become internationally recognized as an organ soloist of exceptional gifts, spent a decade of his career in the Christ Church Cathedral organ loft and was also a memorable, if controversial, master of the choir there. The controversy erupted as a result of English-church-trained Steed's wish to eliminate female voices from the choir, a move which infuriated the ladies and was not popular with then Dean, the Very Reverend Brian Whitlow.

On the female side of choral achievements I remember many fine concerts by the Schubert Club (1923–53), conducted by the indefatigable Frederic King (who had also founded the male voice Meistersingers in 1934), and the Georgian Choristers, conducted by Georgina Watt (Hobbis) from 1936 until at least 1948.

The city can boast several choral groups with long histories. The Victoria Choral Society closed its fiftieth anniversary season in 1985 and the Arion Male Voice Choir has just celebrated its centennial year, having given its first concert on 17 May 1893. Despite many ups and downs over the years, this group was often

38

considered one of the finest male voice choirs in Canada — and is certainly the oldest.

Local choirs provided a ready outlet for vocal soloists, and it was seldom in the early days that one had to look outside the city for artists capable of engaging in even the most demanding of oratorios and cantatas. Among those vocal soloists active in the decade preceding the outbreak of the Second World War were Eva Baird, Lily Wilson, the remarkable soprano and bass husband-and-wife team of Thelma and Harry Johns, Constance Tyrwhitt-Drake, and Eleanor Duff, whose rich contralto was likened by Cathedral organist Graham Steed to Britain's memorable Kathleen Ferrier.

The presence of professional teachers of singing, who were often attached to local choral organizations as conductors, resulted in the development of many local singing personalities. Irene Byatt was an outstanding teenage contralto whose splendid voice was first publicly revealed at a Sir James Douglas School Parent-Teacher Association concert. The PTA made her a protégé, providing her with tuition fees for study and other essentials. After a few years she left Victoria and in time became established at Canada's Stratford Festival and now works mainly out of Los Angeles. John Dunbar, the popular baritone and stage personality, was one of the many students of Roberto and Mary Wood who benefited greatly from their instuction. Jock, as he likes to be called, forsook a budding professional touring career in Scotland and Britain for his love of family and life generally in Victoria.

There were many other Victoria singers who were more than competent in operatic roles as well as on the concert stage. Among those I remember best are Eva Hart, Pierre Timp (the velvet-voiced baritone who was particularly effective in lieder), and Peggy Walton Packard, who studied in New York and whose full dramatic soprano was acclaimed as the mother in all but one of the Cathedral's six triennial productions of *Amahl and the Night Visitors*. Of special note are Adele Goult-Lewis, endowed with a soprano voice of such quality that Britain's great teacher, Roy Henderson, offered her a place in his studio, and tenors Charles Dorrington, Norman Tyrrell, and Arthur Wiebe. Among those who have more recently entered the field are Catherine Lewis, Benjamin Butterfield, and Judith Dowling.

The Ladies' Musical Club, in addition to its role as impresario, also provided necessary public performance outlets for budding performers, both vocal and instrumental. The Club, created as the nineteenth century gave way to the twentieth and continuously active for more than fifty years, had a considerable influence on the musical arts in Victoria. Before the arrival of mainland-based impresarios Gordon Hilker and Hugh Pickett, the society was the only organization that brought outstanding artists to Victoria on a regular basis. We were thus able to enjoy such immortals as Charles Wakefield Cadman, John McCormack, Nellie Melba and great Canadians like the incomparable Winnipeg-born violinist Kathleen Parlow together with local performers such as Gertrude Huntly Green and Winifred Lugrin Fahey.

The club was well placed in the social order and its first president was Mrs. James Douglas Helmcken, daughter-in-law of Victoria's pioneer doctor, John Sebastian Helmcken. When the term, "Ladies" came to be considered snobbish and outdated, the club changed its name to the Musical Art Society (1930) and began to sponsor intermediate and junior subsidiaries to encourage young performers. These adjuncts were particularly useful at a period in Victoria when there was no conservatory of music and students in private teaching studios had little chance of sharing their musical experience and knowledge with each other.

Many of the community's benefactors in the arts were associated with the Ladies' Musical Club. Particularly notable were the J. O. Camerons. They were leaders in sponsoring musical talent and making opportunities available to the aspiring young artist, including opening their Moss street home, Roseboro, to young musicians in need of a performing space and an audience.

I especially remember an incident that demonstrates Beatrix Cameron's generosity. She had written a poem entitled *Clouds*, which she wanted to have read at one of her soirées, the reading to be accompanied at the piano by suitable music. I do not remember the name of the reader, but it was probably someone from the late Mrs. Wilfrid Ord's speech studio — perhaps her daughter, Clemency. I had been asked to provide the accompaniment and, having read the poem and absorbed its atmosphere and delicacy, I decided to play a Debussy *Prelude*. Both of us considered being asked to perform at Roseboro a privilege and an honour and thus expected no compensation. After the event was over Mrs. Cameron, with emotion, presented each of us with a sterling silver compact, worth more than several weeks of arts journalism assignments.

The J. O. Cameron Pavilion in Beacon Hill Park, where concerts have been performed throughout the summers since its completion, is a memorial to the generosity of both James Oscar and Beatrix and their sponsorship of the musical presence in the city.

Space, an instrument, and an audience were quite frequently provided for soirées or matinées by others of the city's wealthy and culture-oriented citizens. Among them were Miss Kathleen Agnew in her home on Rockland Avenue and Mrs. Hebden (Mai) Gillespie, the latter a violinist of some ability with an affinity for chamber music enhanced by travels and study abroad. Her dedication to Bach encouraged the formation of a chamber group among her circle of musical friends, and she introduced a Bach class into the local music festival.

These dilettantes gathered about them friends who shared their pleasure in amateur performance. Perhaps most memorable among these was Judge Montague Tyrwhitt-Drake's mother, Constance. She was a large lady with a radiant complexion, a bright, friendly temperament, and a well-placed pleasing voice. Her delicate style and charm were most attractive when she sang selections from her quite extensive French vocal repertoire. All these talented people loved to perform and frequently hosted tea-musicals in their homes, which gave gifted students some of their first opportunities to perform. Those events provided my first introduction to chamber music and ignited a life-long love for it.

Quita (Mrs. Walter) Nichol, widow of a former Lieutenant Governor, also delighted in airing her pleasant, though limited, light soprano voice and also provided performance opportunities for other compatible musical talents among the city's gifted élite. She was a cheerful, attractive, and friendly person. Her only obvious flaw was that, although her voice was only average, she liked more than anything to sing before a captive audience of friends, and she had both the wealth and the social status to make this possible. She was also generous, even to the extent of sharing the limelight on occasion with those considerably more talented. Applause and many compliments were generally showered on the hostess and her guests. Of course there were no carping, ill-natured critics invited — except once.

On that particular afternoon the double drawing room of the Nichol home was filled with friends of the hostess who were especially agog as Constance Tyrwhitt-Drake had been invited to give a brief recital from her charming French repertoire. I was present among a small invited group of teenage music students. Mrs. Nichol, not to be entirely hidden under a bushel, announced that she, upon being urged, would sing a couple of songs. Rose-tinted applause ensued. She also announced that her two young grandsons were being allowed to come in to listen to Grandma sing. Little more than toddlers, they were ushered in by their nanny and seated on footstools at the front of the audience with nanny standing nearby.

Grandma performed an ambitious number, soaring to some particularly high notes well beyond her range. To these she gave her all. The eldest grandson turned to his nanny, demanding loudly: "What is grandma making all that noise for?" This was the first of two occasions on which I was present when a critic was ordered from the scene. On a second occasion, many years later, I was that critic.

The long-established Musical Art Society weathered the war years and still held a high profile after that time, particularly under the guidance of music buff Roger Manning and his successor Mollie Watts. Mrs. Watts was a wealthy woman and devoted herself, until her death and beyond, to the financial sustenance of the organization and especially to its role in aiding gifted and serious music students. The society was also the custodian of a fund to provide vocal bursaries in memory of Ethel James who had been for many years an esteemed Victoria teacher of singing. Eventually the Society ceased its activity but continues to administer the bursary funds into the century's final decade.

In the early days more "educational" work was performed by local organizations such as the Musical Art Society than was available in schools. In my youth the schools were definitely dedicated to tuition based on an old standard curriculum. Any regularized arts education proposal was dismissed as a frill. If some enthusiastic teacher embarked on a musical or a folk-dance programme it all had to be done outside school regular hours. Many children — especially those in schools where the teacher was inspiring — would willingly arrive *en masse* at 8 o'clock in the morning to get in their music, dance practice, or theatre rehearsal before the 9 o'clock bell.

The presence of trained vocal teachers resulted in numerous school choral groups being formed. Classroom choirs from early grades on through junior and senior high school existed throughout the city and also in rural areas. At that time attitudes of school boards towards the arts ranged from disinterest to hostility. At both municipal and provincial government levels there was open antagonism to the idea of accepting music as part of the school curriculum. In spite of this opposition there were many dedicated teachers who understood the developmental influence that music had in young lives and were willing to go beyond regulation classroom hours to train a choir or a band, and, a little later, string groups, orchestras, and to instruct students in the arts of dance and theatre.

Arts training in the high schools was led by such teachers as Norma Douglas of Victoria High School. She was not only talented but had the ability to convey her enthusiasm to her students. Miss Douglas was able to instil acceptance and even enthusiasm among her senior high school boys' choirs. The torch was also carried by Harold Taylor, an inspiring teacher who developed the Victoria High School Orchestra, which would become the Victoria Junior Symphony in the 1930s.

It was a joy to hear these groups and a major disappointment to students, parents, teachers, and the public when it was ordained that such organizations as school orchestras were "élitist" and therefore expendable. After a hiatus of some years it was with the arrival of Dr. J. F. K. English in 1949 that the perception of music within the school system began to alter. English was then Chief Inspector of Schools for the province and both he and his wife, Ada, were deeply interested in music and had been strong supporters of an active music festival in Kamloops before coming here. Both were astonished to learn that there was no music festival in the capital city and little music instruction in the schools. J. F. K. soon became Deputy Minister of Education and through his influence music would once again become an important part of the school curriculum.

Among the leaders in this renewed development was Bernard Rain. A violinist and dedicated strings teacher, he was on the staff at Oak Bay Secondary and formed string groups at the school where both he and his students willingly gave after-hours time to practise. Among others was Dorothy (Hopgood) Evans, music instructor at Victoria High School, who taught many gifted string students and developed what was actually a junior symphony. There were also band directors such as Emil Michaux at Mount Douglas, Howard Denike at Reynolds Junior Secondary, and David Dunnet at Oak Bay Secondary. These were people who were devoted and stretched their duties to the limit, fostering the talent of their students, widening their vision, and increasing their technical expertise with tuition and practise both before and after school hours.

These latter developments were closely paralleled by the formal opening of the University of Victoria in 1963. The first president, Dr. Malcolm Taylor, envisioned UVIC as a fine arts university and some of the first university departments included music, theatre and visual arts.

There was some anxiety at the recently-established Conservatory with respect to the impact the development of a School of Music at UVIC would have. The two entities, however, worked well together for many years. Eventually the conservatory's principal, Robin Wood, became Lansdowne Professor at UVIC's School of Music and, in due course, an honorary doctorate was bestowed on him. Meanwhile, Winifred Wood, always a partner with her husband at both the keyboard and in the development of the Conservatory, steered the course of the Conservatory as vice-principal and extended its reach by establishing a diploma course at Camosun College. This move was well received and showed excellent promise until the generally sagging economy forced a slash in funding and the music diploma course as well as a professional theatre course were cancelled.

Although piano is the "instrument of choice" among young musicians, the Conservatory has not ignored or failed to recognize the pressing need for string players. Heading the violin and cello studios from early days are two of Canada's best teachers — Sidney Humphreys (a violinist internationally noted for his fine chamber music performances) and cellist James Hunter (from whose dedicated teaching have come a number of first-chair cellists around the continent).

Victoria is a city that long held a reputation for enthusiastically welcoming touring opera, musical comedy, and ballet companies. Soaring costs of travel with trunks of costumes, scenery, lighting, and props, however, have radically reduced the capability of "going on the road" for many companies, especially those from overseas. The development of television and movies has had some influence but not to the degree once thought to be inevitable.

Now only the mega-productions can afford to go on the road and then only with the largest cities as their goals. Cities smaller than Vancouver, Winnipeg, Ottawa, Toronto, and Montreal must count themselves fortunate when they possess their own competent production groups. Victoria has shown a strong loyalty to its two oldest of these — Langham Court's Victoria Theatre Guild whose roots were struck in 1929 and which now presents full seasons regularly to sellout houses, and the Victoria Operatic Society which is approaching its half-century and is still well supported by a dedicated audience that welcomes its repetitions of past apparently deathless favourites such as *Brigadoon, My Fair Lady, Showboat, Man of La Mancha, South Pacific,* and the more recent *Jesus Christ Superstar* and *Godspell* among numerous others.

To this latter strongly rooted and generally competent organization there have been attracted some of the best of local musicians as musical directors and conductors as well as competent, if not always inspired, stage directors, lighting experts, and scenic designers. All of this activity is undertaken for love of the art and defies the pejorative sense in which the word "amateur" is so frequently used.

Of all of these development, however, none is more exciting than the story of the birth and growth of the Victoria Symphony Orchestra, now one of the few orchestras in Canada that can boast a balanced ledger.

CHAPTER SIX

Orchestras

HERE had been for some time among the city's teachers of stringed instruments a few who cherished the dream of putting together an orchestra, a dream not easily accomplished in a town where funds for the arts were not considered a priority. If such funds were to be forthcoming wind bands would almost certainly be the first choice.

Attempts to develop orchestras in Victoria can be traced back as far as the Victoria Amateur Orchestra of 1878, which was directed by Coote Mulloy Chambers. Other attempts at orchestra building were later spearheaded by Emile Pferdner (1885), F. Victor Austin (1898), Frank Watkis (1904), Louis Turner (1910), Georges d'Arnould (1913), and Frank Sehl (1918). The latter ensemble, perhaps the most successful of the early orchestras, was developed in conjunction with eminent Victoria pianist Gertrude Huntly Green (who appeared as both violinist and pianist in the ensemble) and was sometimes referred to as the Red Cross Orchestra because of its financial contributions to that important wartime effort. None of these early orchestras, however, had any degree of longevity.

My own introduction to a string orchestra came as a pre-teenager through Drury Pryce, an Englishman who had previously been an orchestral musician in London and a teacher of strings in Kelowna. Unquestionably knowledgeable in string playing, he had come to Victoria in 1921 where he established a string teaching studio on Fort Street. Soon after establishing his studio Pryce assembled a chamber orchestra utilizing the best of his students and a number of instrumentalists who had gained experience in earlier episodes of ensemble work. He had no difficulty in filling his restricted audience seating at first. I was among a sprinkling of youngsters accompanied by parents, who were mostly members of the Ladies' Musical Club. Most of the comments I heard were of the negative kind.

They referred most particularly to Pryce's sombre manner and the passionless precision he brought to his readings of the scores. Accompanying my mother to these concerts was for me, however, an introduction to instrumental ensemble performance and I was fascinated. My elders could call them "uninspired" but I hoped for more of the same. Dull as they probably were they sowed in me a lifelong taste for orchestral music.

The Victoria Orchestral Society, as the group became known, was conducted from 1925 by Wilfred Willett who was a British expatriate and had organized the Cowichan Orchestral Society in 1916. Willett had studied music as a choirboy at Windsor Castle and had taught at Eton before becoming an insurance and real estate agent in Duncan. He commuted to Victoria on a weekly basis to take rehearsals with the orchestra. In 1927 Willett gave up this orchestra and in the same year Pryce moved to Ottawa where he became music instructor with the Ottawa Board of Education, leaving the orchestral scene in Victoria once again barren.

As the 1930s emerged there were visits by the Seattle Symphony and, on at least two occasions, the Vancouver Symphony came over, reminding us that though we were the province's capital real culture was to be found only on the mainland. Attendance at these concerts suggested that there were enough symphonically-inclined concert-goers to make a resident orchestra a worthwhile undertaking. Seen as further evidence was the popularity of instrumental ensembles such as the HMCS *Naden* Band, and others, which occasionally performed in Beacon Hill Park.

Throughout the grim decade of the thirties young people nearing graduation from high school had no great expectations of finding good jobs, let alone any encouragement in their performance skills. For those musically talented it was a distraction and a fulfilling experience when gifted cellist and school teacher Harold Taylor put together a junior orchestra in 1931 with which he worked devotedly. Following Taylor's death urgent pleas from some of the young players fostered a movement to assemble a symphonic orchestra which was to become the last in a long line of such attempts. The training these teenagers had received from Taylor and the satisfaction they derived from this experience later made them eager material for Alfred Prescott, a local band director who had operated a small amateur orchestra under the name Victoria Philharmonic Society since 1931. Prescott would be known as the founder of the Victoria Symphony Orchestra, which was to become the only orchestral ensemble to have any degree of permanence in the city.

Among those who were in the forefront of organizing this ensemble were Fay Ockenden, Douglas and Denis Kent, Betty Mulliner, and Gilbert Margison. Music ran in the Margison family. His two cousins, Dorothy and Mildred, were pianists and teachers of music and his parents were musically gifted. Gilbert had a young son who showed early musical ability as well as exceptional vocal promise. His name was Richard and he is now the internationally noted Canadian operatic tenor.

Prescott worked hard with the new orchestra, carrying it forward to the extent that technical and monetary resources allowed. The latter were modest indeed by present standards. An ambitious and well-received concert was given at the Royal Victoria Theatre on 12 April 1939, with Fay Ockenden as concert mistress. Her accomplished pianist sister, Helen, performed the Grieg *Piano Concerto* and orchestral numbers included Beethoven's *Symphony No. Five* and Sibelius's *Finlandia*. Responding to enthusiastic applause, Prescott announced the intention of presenting a full season of orchestral music starting that fall.

But there was not to be a season nor even a second concert before the Second World War flared over Europe. Aside from the executive committee the Victoria Symphony Orchestra had no real support structure. Nevertheless, Prescott had assembled an orchestral resource pool that indicated that both the talent and the will were present. Two years were to pass before an ambitious and untried but business-wise young conductor came on the scene and there was a new beginning.

Melvin Knudsen was a Danish cabinet maker, tall, thin, dark, and probably in his middle to late thirties when I first knew him. Fine carpentry was his livelihood but his mindset was music. Possessing some musical education, he was hypnotically drawn to the orchestral podium, so much so that hearing of a conducting course being presented in Switzerland by famed maestro Fritz Weingartner, Knudsen downed the tools of his trade and took off in pursuit of his constant dream.

After several weeks he returned and knew that more than anything else in the world he wanted to conduct an orchestra. Being practical as well as being a dreamer, he also knew that no genie or fairy godmother was going to conjure one up for him. Aware that most of the group of musicians who had comprised Prescott's orchestra were still available, he set out to make his dream a reality. Pragmatic as he was by nature, he could not imagine that his pursuit would lay the foundation stone of what, half a century later, would be recognized as the city's leading cultural asset.

He wisely went to work first on the subject of finances. Among the many things he had learned in Europe was that all arts organizations, if they are to survive and achieve an acceptable artistic level, must have in place a dependable and constant financial structure. He chose initially to approach Sam Clack, the Estates Manager of the Victoria branch of Royal Trust. Knudsen found in him a sympathetic listener. His carefully thought out approach to the undertaking and his enthusiasm convinced Mr. Clack and activity was soon underway toward establishing a symphony orchestra by the fall of 1941. Former members of the short-lived Prescott orchestra were quick to grasp the opportunity. A committee was formed with Naval Volunteer Reserve Officer Lieutenant R. Hartie as president and French hornist Douglas Kent as vice-president. The knowledgeable finance committee assembled by Mr. Clack consisted of Warren Martin, Sara Spencer (daughter of the Spencer family), and himself. The initial budget was set at $1,000 which was then, for

Victoria, a perfectly reasonable start-up amount for a predominantly amateur orchestra.

The new orchestra was somewhat of a reincarnation, the personnel including basically those from Prescott's time with Fay Ockenden again as concert mistress. One or two vacant chairs in the winds section were filled by musicians from the HMCS *Naden* Band stationed at Esquimalt. An early fall beginning allowed the ensemble to rehearse under Knudsen throughout the winter months in preparation for the first concert of the new organization, more than two years after its birth.

The new Victoria Symphonic Orchestra, as it was first called, made its bow in the Empress Hotel Ballroom on 18 May 1942. The room was full of music lovers eager to hear and assess this latest endeavour. There were the optimists prepared for its success and willing to believe in its future and there were those who made up the majority — the pragmatists whose attitude, while friendly, was sceptical. They gave it, at most, two years, suspecting that it might not even survive the war.

As it turned out the war years were easier for the orchestra to negotiate than the peace that followed. For one thing there was the problem of changes in naval personnel after the war which resulted in a withdrawal of certain *Naden* musicians from this activity. The major loss was experienced in the brass section and, to a lesser extent, among the woodwinds. Any absence of naval band players, as when the band went on tour, meant the extra expense of bringing competent brass and woodwind players from Vancouver to fill their places. Still, the orchestra continued into its fifth year backed by a dedicated board headed, after Lieutenant Hartie's departure, by Miss Sara Spencer. Music ran deep in the Wales-rooted Spencer family, even for a time luring Myfanwy (Pavelic), the talented daughter of Will Spencer, to contemplate the career of a pianist rather than that of a portrait artist which was to bring her international acclaim.

Early public support for the symphony had developed beyond expectation and it soon became obvious that the Empress Ballroom was too small to make even modest allowance for the growing audience. The orchestra moved into the Royal Theatre in the fall of 1943 but, despite the enthusiastic reception accorded the concerts, income continued to be less than expenditure. This is, even today, a common problem with all arts organizations.

A dedicated women's committee was formed in 1948 with sculptor Elza Mayhew as its first president. This committee has worked continuously through the years providing unfailing financial aid by undertaking a variety of ambitious money-making activities. One of the most successful of these were the annual dinner-balls at the Empress which, unfortunately, ended when styles of dance music changed and younger generations were no longer interested. Its attraction was also greatly diminished for those whose special delight had been the first hour in which the symphony itself, playing Strauss waltzes and polkas, was the dance orchestra. What followed for the rest of the evening was a hired band which the majority of members and guests enjoyed. Full-dress openings of Victoria Symphony Orchestra (vso) seasons were also promoted for a time in early days but this soon ceased to be the custom.

Early in the establishment of the women's committee I was given *carte blanche* to attend those meetings in order to obtain information for articles I was writing. Because of this I came to fully understand the problems of operating a symphony society. The main problem was — still is and probably will be forever — that ticket prices cannot be set at an amount sufficient to cover all the costs incurred in mounting a concert series. Raising prices to a level that would cover all costs would put the concerts out of reach of much of the public. It was firmly established in the vso code over the ensuing decades, as it is now virtually worldwide, that music is for everyone, not just the wealthy and socially prominent.

In the early years only first chair players, guest artists, and the conductor, received remuneration. This could not go on indefinitely without diminishing the quality of the product, but there was undoubted hostility in Victoria at the time towards the idea of paying symphony musicians, particularly among city and municipal council members .

Indeed, among entrenched musical organizations up to the dawn of the seventies there existed the attitude that resident performers on any instrument were somehow vulgar and unworthy if they made it plain that they had set a price on their performance. Visitors from neighbouring cities might logically receive a fee but the natives were expected to supply their talents for love alone. This attitude changed slowly but maintained a high profile at City Hall for many years. Some mayors and many aldermen — although there were notable exceptions — were strongly of the opinion that symphony instrumentalists should be satisfied "with the pleasure of performing." For that matter the consensus was that any art should not expect to be supported out of the public purse. Such organizations as orchestras and theatre companies — to say nothing of art galleries — were regarded as luxuries and therefore élitist. Those who had chosen to follow their particular talents and love for music, theatre, or any other art, should not expect others to pay for their indulgence. That was the unspoken but strongly indicated attitude of many, the openly expressed opinion of only a few.

One day I received a call from a woman whose organization was presenting in concert a singer from Vancouver. The singer's accompanist had come down with 'flu. My caller had tried one or two local pianists both of whom were busy on that particular night and wondered if I could help her. I asked if she had contacted Malcolm Hamilton, an accomplished young man who played both piano and harpsichord and possessed that quite rare gift, the sensitive art of accompaniment. "Yes, I've called him," she exclaimed indignantly, "but he wants to be paid!"[1]

At the end of his seventh season with the Victoria Symphony Knudsen stepped down from the podium, having brought the orchestra some distance past its originally prophesied life expectancy of two years. The relationship between the conductor and his musi-

---

[1] Later Malcolm Hamilton was to move to California where he became piano and harpsichord accompanist to renowned violinist Jascha Heifetz. Together they made a number of fine recordings.

cians, however, had deteriorated, in part because of the shallowness of Knudsen's serious musical knowledge. This perceived criticism was really to his credit for he had, by this time, gathered around him musicians of considerable expertise. The board was made aware that many of the better musicians would be leaving the orchestra unless a more experienced and qualified conductor was appointed.

There were those among the audiences who expressed shock and some indignation when word got around that Knudsen was being replaced. Many regarded the symphony as "his" orchestra, ignoring the fact that a short course of training on the podium without a lengthy and in-depth study of musical styles and repertoire was unlikely to produce an inspired or even a competent conductor.

As the eighth season approached Knudsen was replaced by Hans Gruber, a young musician from Toronto who was highly recommended by the late Sir Ernest McMillan, then head of the University of Toronto School of Music. Gruber had conducted only the student orchestra at the university but had shown a keen musical intellect and sense of style. He was to remain on the Victoria podium for 15 years.

These were years that involved considerable growth in both the number and quality of the personnel as well as some important innovations. To the regular season at the Royal, out-of-town concerts and the memorable summer series at Butchart Gardens were added. These were the inspiration of, and sponsored by, Butchart owners Ian and Ann-Lee Ross (Ian is the grandson of the Gardens' original designer and creator, Jenny Butchart). The setting for the orchestra — the gardens' rich floral beauty, sheltered lawns, and gentle flower-scented breezes — attracted audiences of somewhere between 3,000 to 5,000 persons for each event.

Gruber's tenure was the longest of any conductor who led the Victoria Symphony over the following twenty-five years. Through his leadership many important moves were made by dedicated boards headed, after Sara Spencer's term, by Walter Stenner and then by Dr. J. F. K. English. Alix (Mrs. Massy) Goolden served the Symphony Society board with distinction and accustomed generosity for many years.

This era is further memorable for the significant presence and activity of yet another key figure — Jack Barraclough. When he arrived in Victoria from the mainland in 1932 Jack was already involved in the insurance business and noted for his organizational capabilities. As a youth in his native Yorkshire he had fallen in love with orchestral music and used to save up his pocket money to buy tickets for orchestra concerts. Jack and his wife, Kay (Kathleen), immediately started attending Victoria Symphony concerts. Both became involved with the business end, Kay joining the Women's Committee (of which she was later a president) and Jack being elected to the board.

It was not long before he occupied the president's chair, remaining in that position for ten years of steady growth. During his tenure the vso never ended a season "in the red." When money was needed Jack could always find it. After he stepped down from the presidency he continued on the board for a total of twenty-seven years. Although she preferred to stay in the background, Barraclough had a staunch ally in Mrs. Goolden, whose love of music was balanced by her continuing support for local charitable ventures such as the Protestant Orphanage. Both were also involved in fundraising for another landmark project, the Victoria Conservatory of Music.

Although the music school was originally his idea, by 1965 Gruber had left the Symphony podium to return to Toronto. There seemed no doubt, however, that the orchestra's next conductor should be willing to step in as the new school's principal.

The new conductor was Otto-Werner Mueller, six-foot-seven, lean, imperious, and a musical genius. Born in Germany, he had emigrated to Canada after the war and, until coming to Victoria, he had lived in Montreal. There he had been a conductor for the cbc in addition to other musical activities. Mueller agreed to head the new school in addition to his role as symphony conductor. Midway through his stay — it was the briefest of the six conductors who directed the Victoria Symphony from 1942 to the early 1990s — I consulted him one day on the choice of an opera to be included in a proposed summer festival programme. I told him that the proposers were thinking of Verdi's *La Traviata*. He countered with *The Barber of Seville*, pointing out the additional expense of training and costuming the chorus for *Traviata*. Then he added that in a few weeks he would be flying back to Montreal to conduct the final rehearsals for the CBC production of *The Barber*, the first complete opera televised by that network. He suggested I come along to see what is involved in a televised opera production.

The idea enthralled me, not only for the experience that it would provide, but it would also likely result in some good column material on my return. Stu Keate was still publisher of the paper, a strong supporter of the arts and always ready to listen to innovative ideas. I went to him with the proposition and he immediately endorsed it, all expenses paid. Later he was also to endorse my request to attend the opening of the new Festival Theatre at Stratford, Ontario.

It was my first visit to Montreal and I had little time for sightseeing. At the CBC studio my presence was taken in stride by the stage director and crew who placed me in advantageous positions from which to watch the progress of the rehearsals. When Don Basilio sang the brilliant aria, "La Calumnia," in which he describes to Rosina's guardian the mischief that could be done to her lover by spreading gossip abroad, he was sitting in front of a hearth which was open not only towards the cameras, but at the back with a real fire blazing. There I was, warming my toes on the off-camera side and revelling in a close-up of Don Basilio's superb facial language.

Every night at the end of rehearsals we all went off to some pub and sat drinking wine or beer, eating crusty bread and cheese, and indulging in lively dialogue until the early morning hours. Satire and thinly-veiled political commentary highlighted the conversation from time to time, none more good-humouredly challenging than the moment when Otto commented to French-Canadian baritone Louis Quilico: "This is Audrey Johnson's first visit to Montreal." Quilico turned to me with a grin, extended his hand, and said: "Welcome to Canada!"

56

The event which precipitated Mueller's departure in 1967 involved a remark delivered offhandedly following a council meeting at City Hall. A committee from the Victoria Symphony was visiting Council to present a request for a modest special-purpose grant — somewhere in the neighbourhood of $3000 — and was summarily turned down. It happened that one alderman was overheard by a *Times* city-hall reporter saying something to the effect that he was "sick and tired of these people coming here hat-in-hand like beggars." The slur hit the front page headline the next day and lit a flash-fire under Mueller who immediately resigned as Symphony conductor and School of Music principal. Taking the rebuff as a personal insult, he declared: "I refuse to continue to live and work in a city that considers me a beggar."

There were musically-alert people who mourned the departure of an artist they recognized as a giant, not only physically but also intellectually. It was almost hypnotic to watch him conduct, the long-fingered supple left hand conjuring subtleties and shapes in sound and phrase from players, many of whom had never previously encountered such musical comprehension. In many ways Mueller was quite obviously a man before his time for Victoria. Those members of the orchestra who were less than fluent technically found him lacking in patience and harsh in criticism. He also had little skill and no patience in dealing at the social level. One inane comment overheard from a person close to the Symphony Society core was that "at least we might now get a conductor who would be acceptable at Government House."

Otto-Werner Mueller was, heart and soul, a man of music. Other than his wife and two sons it was all that mattered to him. He enjoyed a few close friends among whom were my husband and good-natured Arne Bo, a violist with the orchestra who doubled as symphony manager until he left to follow Otto to the United States.

Now and then Otto would spend an evening in our home over a bottle of scotch discussing a broad panorama of subjects — history in general, and German history in particular, referring only occasionally to the Nazi regime, which he despised. The scotch would be significantly lowered by the end of the session without noticeable effect on either host or guest. Otto's big frame could absorb a generous amount without apparent effect and Maurice could always make a single measure, topped up now and then with soda, last out the evening.

The Victoria Symphony personnel of the sixties was two-thirds non-professional and much of it — even some of the professionals — were not wholly secure in pitch and certainly not hardened to the tough, unremitting discipline and technical agility to which an orchestra conducted by Mueller must aspire. The result was that some of the players became disheartened and resentful. It is even possible that if Mueller had stayed on there would have been a serious number of resignations from the orchestra.

Mueller returned to Victoria only once to fulfill a commitment to conduct a performance of Verdi's *Requiem.* An augmented choir consisting of the Victoria Choral Society, the new University of Victoria School of Music choir, and other experienced local ensemble singers joined the group. The inspired performance turned out to be a landmark event in the city's presentation of great choral works. Otto-Werner Mueller then returned to the United States with his wife and two young sons, climbing rapidly to significant status as an orchestral expert and a notable teacher. Currently he is head of the orchestral section of the Curtis Institute in Philadelphia.

Mueller's two seasons were as much as anything a revelation of what might be possible given time and sufficient funding. They were as though a window were briefly opened to reveal a glimpse of more splendid things hidden in the middle distance. His passion for the music itself outweighed any other consideration including his players' feelings. One night a rehearsal I attended was not going at all to his liking in the string section. Tapping his stand to stop the action, he turned on the cellos: "You play like *pigs*!" he told them disgustedly. He may have given vent to his own frustration but scarcely encouraged the struggling amateurs to try harder.

Before Mueller left he recommended a young Hungarian conductor working in Montreal, Laszlo Gati, to the board. Gati was a conductor who effortlessly brought great warmth and romanticism to his interpretations. While he had greater sympathy for his musicians than Mueller and created a happier atmosphere backstage, he also often stirred emotions to a steaming boil in his association with the board and its individual members.

Gati's musicianship, however, was admirable. His principal gift to the orchestra was a certain sensitizing, a romanticism that lifted even the most average player into imaginative realms beyond the undoubted necessary struggle for technical mastery. He was especially successful in bringing that message to children when the orchestra visited schools and participated with Kaleidoscope Theatre in presenting vivid imaginative interpretations of the music.

Gati empathised closely with the young in a way that suggested he had never waved a final farewell to his own youthful years. He could glory in his popular presence on the podium, preen himself when the sun shone on his efforts, and stamp around and fume when he didn't get his own way. His principal annoyance for the board was his habit of turning up at board meetings unannounced and uninvited and precipitating himself into the middle of discussions concerning what they defined, for the most part accurately, as purely board business.

Nevertheless, Gati's ten-year stay (1967–78) included much that was sensitive and lyrical and, to the extent of which the players were capable, at times spirited. He also made use of summer evenings by establishing summer evening concerts in the Royal Victoria Museum courtyard outside the Newcombe Theatre.

When his tenure ended there followed a "year of the maestros" during which everybody — board, orchestra personnel, and audiences — got a shot at voting for their favourite among a procession of guest conductors. This proved to be neither a satisfactory nor a sensible procedure and it was abandoned on the next occasion. The overall choice of the board turned out to be the last contender in the "lottery," Dr. Paul Freeman. Freeman was a man of flamboyant personality and was dedicated to building an international career. He was young enough to have retained the exuberance of youth and sufficient vigour to wing his way about the globe when required. The Victoria Symphony provided him with a means towards his personal goal while at the same time having a national and international spotlight turned upon himself and his orchestra.

In the eight seasons of his reign (1979–88) Freeman was able to lure the hitherto evasive Canadian Broadcasting Corporation into crossing the hitherto seemingly impassable Georgia Strait — not once, but twice — to record VSO concerts and subsequently to broadcast them Canada-wide. Closely aligned with his personal ambition was his organizing of the orchestra's only two major tours in its history, one through the BC interior to Alaska and another south through the Pacific coastal states to California, the latter culminating in a well-received concert in San Francisco. The first commercial recordings made by the orchestra were also produced during Freeman's conductorship.

Freeman's bounding ebullient personality and the excitement he could arouse when conducting some of his favourite South American and other high-powered rhythmic compositions, made him a favourite with a large percentage of his audiences. Behind the scenes, however, the situation was quite different. Empathy between conductor and players — not always formerly present by any means but desirable nevertheless — was not good and finally broke down. While there is no law nor tradition that says a conductor and his players must be friends it is vital that respect be mutual. In any such alignment respect is the principal key to successful artistic functioning, whether it be director and actors, conductor and ensemble, or choreographer and dancers.

Freeman's departure for Chicago, where he immediately established his own small orchestra, was lamented by much of his Victoria audience. Another season of guest conductors followed but this time the decision to hire was, wisely, left in the hands of a joint committee consisting of representatives from the board and orchestra.

This time not all that season's visiting conductors were candidates for the position of artistic director but of those who expressed interest the choice, by a wide margin, was clearly Peter McCoppin. Personable, without the flamboyance of an abounding ego, sincere and perceptive in his musical approach, McCoppin came from Vancouver where he had been credited with resurrecting the then comatose Vancouver Symphony and restoring it to its rightful place among Canadian orchestras. McCoppin was the first conductor for some years to interact warmly with his musicians.

McCoppin's style is quite contrary to the more familiar carica-ture of the orchestral conductor — bounding onto the podium and taking all the glory and the praise. Rather, on returning to the stage, McCoppin moves among the orchestra players beckoning certain sections to rise and applauding them from the sidelines along with the audience. He concludes by turning to the audience, smilingly acknowledging the applause as he shares it, not on a superior level, but as one of the ensemble. Sensitive and charismatic, McCoppin has healed wounds and, with his relaxed manner, meticulous con-ducting style, and clear musicianship, created an ideal relationship in which friction no longer erodes accomplishment.

While boards have changed, managers have come and gone, and numerous internal crises have arisen over the years, the orches-tra has had a capable associate music director in Glen Fast. A sensitive musician, Fast has maintained a constant, reliable pres-ence on the podium. His is an essential role in orchestras where the principal conductor inevitably has external commitments taking him from the city several times during the season. The role of associate conductor is particularly vital where the growth has been as exten-sive as that of the Victoria Symphony Orchestra. During the regular season, besides twelve Masterworks pairs, the orchestra currently presents a classic series of six pairs of chamber works, six pops concerts, a series of children's concerts, and annual perform-ances of *Messiah* in association with the Victoria Choral Society. In addition to this the orchestra serves with Pacific Opera productions three times each season and there is often a summer season.

Members of the orchestra are engaged during the summer with the Johannesen International Festival and, starting in the summer of 1990 (just a year short of VSO's fiftieth anniversary) it revived the presentation of open-air concerts that had been initiated by Gruber at Butchart Gardens and revived by Gati in the Provincial Museum courtyard.

Having mounted a hugely successful July 1990 concert on a moored barge in the Inner Harbour that was attended by 33,000 people, the Symphony Society repeated this immense public event in 1991 and, in addition, added a short August series. All were enthusiastically attended, the harbour concert soaring beyond its previous record to close to 38,000. By 1993 this audience had swelled to almost 45,000.

Each of the six conductors who have so far stepped onto the Victoria Symphony podium have contributed in some particular way to the orchestra's development. As time passed the VSO continued to become better known over a wider area and the financial picture, while it had its ups and downs, began to look brighter. By the end of Gruber's fifteen-year stay (1959) a system of guarantors and donors had been established and grants were being received from the Canada Council, municipal and provincial governments, and the Vancouver Foundation.

However, by the mid-eighties the financial situation was once again more critical. The tenacity and progress that had marked the preceding years had not been without stumbles and mistaken judgements. The financial problems, mostly occurred after the Barraclough years, creating upheavals that more than once threatened the society with sudden death. End-of-season blues were endemic as the continuing deficit crept up despite a wide range of corporate sponsors who had come aboard during the Gati and Freeman regimes.

Back in 1980 the society had been faced by an important decision: whether to convert the orchestra into a fully professional body. At that time it was semi-professional, meaning that only a core segment was engaged on an annual salary basis, the rest being paid hourly rates. A related decision was whether or not to lower the sights as to size from symphony to chamber orchestra as a result of the increased cost of professional status for the musicians.

In 1985-86, when the accumulated deficit was riding at more than $200,000, hobbling the Society and threatening imminent disaster, a new board was elected with Andrew Maxwell as president. With expert financial help a committee was established that began looking for every conceivable way of cutting the fat. At this crucial moment in the Society's affairs a bequest of $60,000 was made to the Victoria Symphony Society to aid in reducing the accumulated deficit. Under ordinary circumstances these funds would have been rerouted to the Victoria Symphony Foundation. The boards of both institutions, however, agreed that its best use was to follow the testator's instructions and apply the bequest towards diminishing the crippling deficit.

The firm commitment of the new board was to carve back the budget, to end the season with a break-even balance, and to improve the financial situation of the orchestra personnel. All of which was accomplished as the year 1990 approached. With the deficit eliminated and ensuing seasons tailored to a break-even position the Victoria Symphony, assisted by a long list of sponsors and hundreds of dedicated private donors, entered the new decade and its 50th anniversary year with confidence.

Closely allied to the story of the Victoria Symphony Orchestra is that of the Conservatory of Music, which grew out of the aspirations of one of the symphony's conductors, and was put on its feet by yet another.

CHAPTER SEVEN

Victoria Conservatory of Music

ONE morning in the early 1960s, Jack Barraclough, chairman of the symphony board, and Hans Gruber, the conductor, were sitting over coffee discussing the difficulty of maintaining the orchestra's ranks at reasonable strength. Most specifically string players were a scarce commodity. Hans commented that this was a problem in many regional orchestras. Gruber suggested that what was needed in Victoria was a school of music for training young players. He felt there were lots of talented youngsters quite ready to go into that kind of special training facility.

The suggestion kindled a flame in Barraclough. It took him little time to draw together a small committee comprising Alix Goolden and other friends and launch a low-profile campaign to put a conservatory fund together. It was not until 1964 that they had accumulated a pool of sufficient proportions to allow them to formally announce the launching of the school, but by that time Hans Gruber, the inspiration for the idea, had returned to Toronto.

One evening at a gathering of some 40 or 50 interested people the announcement was made that the School of Music was poised for takeoff. With Otto-Werner Mueller, the new symphony conductor, as director, a faculty of string and wind teachers had committed themselves, some instruments had been loaned or given, and only a few somewhat important things were still lacking — roof and walls.

Sitting at the back of the room with pad and pencil as the lone representative of the press, I couldn't help thinking that the missing factor was of more than secondary importance. Some remotely possible and some pretty wild suggestions came forth from the audience. These ranged from an elderly vacant mansion situated well off bus routes, a downtown office building (mostly empty and in need of repair), to a vacant former Safeway store at the Oak Bay Junction. The meeting paused and mulled over the Safeway proposal. I held my breath while someone sketched out how the store space could be divided into cells for teaching or practise. In my ears rang the cacophony of sound emerging from this arrangement. However, common sense prevailed and the gathering dispersed with no solution. At that crucial moment the "exceptional memory" for which I had been from time to time commended failed me.

It was not until I was in the office next morning, concentrating on a report of the meeting, that a phone call from several months earlier popped into my mind. It had been from a union secretary who told me that combined unions had recently erected their own building on Quadra Street and wanted to know if any of the theatre or music groups I wrote about would like to have their former building. He described the hall, which was on Pandora Street opposite the McPherson Playhouse, as of concrete block construction with a small auditorium and lots of office space.

I replied that practically everyone involved in the arts dreamed of possessing such a space but presumably the cost would be considerably in excess of annual rental for a church basement or other hall. It would. End of discussion.

Wondering if, by any slim chance, it was still on the market I passed the information on to Jack who said he would follow it up. About a week later I had the word — Mrs. Goolden had bought the building and turned it over to the school of music for as long as it was needed. Thus, as first envisioned by Hans and Jack, the school was underway. It began with 40 students and in the course of 15 years grew steadily until it had completely outgrown the Pandora site.

Gertrude Huntly Green (then Mrs. J. Durand) was always a strong supporter of the music school concept. Her belief in its importance was as firm as her admiration for the teaching of the late Stanley Shale and the superb musicianship of his most illustrious student, Robin Wood. When Otto-Werner Mueller left both the orchestra and the conservatory in 1966 over what he considered a "slap in the face" from Victoria City Council[1] the subject of a new principal became critical.

Robin Wood had been discovered at the age of 10 in a performance at a junior musical club concert and was brought under Stanley Shale's tuition through a patron who recognized his exceptional talent. He would go on to win many festival awards before graduating from the Royal Schools examinations with a scholarship to the Royal Academy of Music and the gold medal for all of Canada. Travelling by ship to England, he met his wife-to-be, Winnipeg pianist Winifred Scott, also heading for the RAM on a scholarship.

Knowing Robin and Winifred Scott now to be on the teaching staff of the Royal Academy, Durand made a private approach by overseas telephone to Robin. Would he consider returning to Victoria to head the new school? His answer, after consultation with his wife, was yes. Within a few days, however, that answer was more tentative. Both the Woods were members of the Royal Academy piano faculty and upon learning they were considering resignation the Academy promptly offered Robin the position of vice-principal.

The couple thought it over for a few days and then cabled Mrs. Durand. They had decided to accept the Victoria School of Music's dual offer of principal and vice-principal. Robin and Winifred were giving up prestigious teaching appointments and interesting professional performance opportunities to return to Victoria. Robin had, for instance, his own chamber ensemble that included the violinist Sidney Humphreys and and his brother the violist Smyth Humphreys. Both Robin and Winifred also had frequent BBC engagements as soloists and duo-pianists. In an interview Robin later remarked that he couldn't face the paper work he would be expected to handle as a vice-principal at the RAM. In addition, their first child was a toddler and both felt that Victoria would provide a healthier environment for children than London.

---

[1] See page 57.

Theirs was a decision that initiated a completely new concept and amazing growth for the School resulting in its reputation spreading rapidly across the Straits into the western provinces and beyond. Gertrude Durand's independent action in making direct contact with Robin Wood is part of the legacy this fine artist left to the city.

Within a comparatively short time the School had outgrown the Pandora Street home, and as growth showed no signs of slowing, it became necessary to seek new quarters. Alix Goolden, then president of the board, together with John Graeme, an active and influential board member, persuaded Mayor Hugh Stephen and the City Council to allow the Conservatory to move into Craigdarroch Castle in 1969.

This move was not popular with the city's earnest historians who were shuddering at the possibility of damage to handsome interior woodwork and plaster. Craigdarroch had already been used as a wartime hospital, was the first location of Victoria College before the latter moved into the former Provincial Normal School (now the Lansdowne Campus of Camosun College), and as the Greater Victoria School Board offices,.

The music school flourished in its new location and continued to branch out, after a time forging a link with the new but rapidly developing University of Victoria School of Music. With this alliance the Victoria School of Music became the Victoria Conservatory of Music. While this formal alliance later broke down, cooperation between the two entities was to be strengthened in another way when Robin became a Lansdowne Professor at UVIC in 1979. He retaining his status with the Conservatory as Professor Emeritus while Winifred assumed the role of principal of the Conservatory. The Conservatory soon established a music course leading to a teaching diploma in conjunction with Camosun College. This welcome and promising addition to the College curriculum unfortunately fell victim to the cost-cutting of the early 1990s. Through most of this period of growth and change the guitarist and lutenist Denis Donnelly has been the administrative director.

Instruction is available on most instruments at the Conservatory, the curriculum including strings, winds, vocal and choral tuition, as well as the essential theory and rudiments of music, harmony and composition. Theory instruction was co-ordinated and taught for many years by Rodney Webster, one of the original staff members and a gifted choral conductor.

Inevitably, with the principals' positions being occupied by two fine pianists, the original concept of emphasis on instruction in orchestral instruments was somewhat modified. Nevertheless, two fine teachers and performers — violinist Sidney Humphreys and cellist James Hunter — became department heads and many orchestras across Canada today have graduates of the Conservatory in their string sections. Some other notable teachers who have served the school over the years include Murray Adaskin (violin), Jack Kessler (violin), Arthur Polson (violin), Hans Siegrist (cello), Katherine Solose (piano), Ilona Bartalus (theory), and Alexander Dunn (guitar). Later, the Suzuki method of teaching violin to pre-schoolers and the Carl Orff "Music for Children" method were introduced.

There was also a growing voice department of the Conservatory. It had become the hothouse from which emerged the expertise that was to combine, grow, and evolve into one of this city's most incredible success stories, the Pacific Opera. Catherine Young, a performer/teacher with professional experience and a graduate of the Eastman School of Music in New York, succeeded Catherine Wendol as head of the Voice Department in 1971. Her ambition was to re-establish opera in Victoria, and to this end she created the Opera Department at the Conservatory in the early 1970s. Her successes were numerous. The first production in the main salon of Craigdarroch Castle (which served as the school's recital and concert hall) was Menotti's *The Medium*. Ideally suited to the Victorian Gothic interior of the castle, it showcased two promising young singers: mezzo-soprano Judy Temple and soprano Pieranne Moon. This was followed by the "Eve of Opera," a series of one-act operas directed by Dale Reed and presented at the old Phoenix Theatre on the UVIC campus during the summer of 1972. In 1974 Young stepped down as the head of the Opera Department, turning it over to Selena James who she had earlier invited to join the voice faculty. James, an artist-teacher with professional operatic experience, headed the department for some years and also now spends part of each year at the Banff School of Fine Arts.

The voice department has had some noted successes among its students, perhaps the most widely known graduates being the international operatic tenor Richard Margison, and Ingrid Attrot, who has launched a professional career based in London, England. There have been several other outstanding singing talents in this city for whom professional careers have seemed a logical expectation, but which, for one reason or another, have not materialized. Any young singer with a better than average vocal potential will only fulfil the promise by finding not only a "good" teacher but the "right" teacher, the voice being a living instrument of great individuality and not a separate creature of wood or metal.

Finally there came a time when continuing growth — the school having passed the one thousand level in student population — led the top teachers to protest the inadequate facilities at Craigdarroch and conditions so restrictive that they made satisfactory teaching impossible. A string teacher was outraged when he found the only "studio" available was nothing more than a janitorial storage area.

Once more rescue came from government when BC Provincial Secretary Hugh Curtis arranged for the school to move into the provincially owned St. Ann's Academy Annex, situated on Academy Close between the main building and Beacon Hill Park. This building had been originally erected to house the convent's primary school.

As a rule, few buildings not planned and erected for a specific purpose work to the complete satisfaction of that purpose. From the outset it was apparent to those with experience of such "temporary" facilities that this one had some serious flaws. There was no space that could be in any way converted into an appropriate small recital hall, for example. On the presentation-day tour I made what appeared to be a tactical error by muttering a low-key reference to the fact that the absence of any space large enough to serve adequately for recitals was going to be detrimental unless someone could come up with a solution. The immediate response from one of the group was: "They're very lucky to get this place — surely they can get by without the luxury of a recital hall"!

I could have presented many arguments in favour of the amenity, including the fact that a conservatory of music is supposed to be, among other things, a place where serious students have the continuing opportunity of hearing fellow students and teachers perform. It should be obvious that all singers and instrumentalists of serious intent must be able to acquire the essential self-control and concentration derived from frequent performance before an audience of fellow students, faculty, and anyone interested, before launching a career. They should be able not only to hear their own instrument, but a whole range of instruments and styles in order to develop a broad perspective of the world of music.

This is particularly true in the case of orchestral instruments. It is, in fact, a main advantage over private study. The conservatory or university school of music provides, for the serious student, familiarity with strings, brass, woodwinds, percussion, and other instruments in addition to his or her own, greatly broadening prospects for future professional undertakings such as qualifying for an orchestral or school teaching position. Realization of that aspect was brought home to me with wind instruments for instance. It was necessary for me, a pianist, to go to the music section of the library, supplementing reading with recordings, and close attention to festival adjudications, in order to make any discerning comments regarding performances on such instruments.

In its new quarters the Victoria Conservatory of Music continues to cope with an enrolment of more than a thousand students each year including those who want to learn only for their own pleasure as well as the earnest pursuers of academic excellence and qualifying diplomas. The music festival movements in the city provided these students with healthy competition as well as inspiration for further development.

The Victoria Symphony performing at Butchart's Gardens in the 1950s. (Victoria *Times-Colonist*)

The Victoria Symphony Orchestra performs at the J. O. Cameron Memorial Pavilion, Beacon Hill Park, July 1972. (John McKay, Victoria *Times-Colonist*)

Maestro Laszlo Gati conducts the Victoria Symphony at Beaver Lake Park, June 1977. (Victoria *Times-Colonist*)

The Victoria Symphony Orchestra performs with David Foster on the steps of the Legislative Buildings, August 1987. (Bart van Herwaarden, Victoria *Times-Colonist*)

Dr. Robin Wood, Principal Emeritus of the Victoria Conservatory of Music with student Patricia McFarlane, 1991 (Victoria Conservatory of Music)

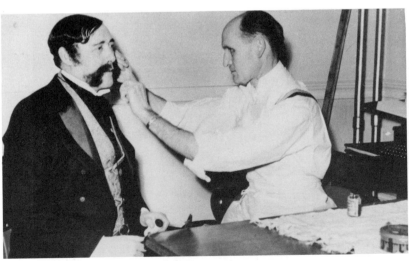

A. M. D. Fairbairn puts finishing touches on the makeup of W. H. Brimblecombe (as Governor Blanchard) for the December 1943 production of *Victoria Cavalcade*. (Victoria Theatre Guild)

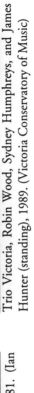

Trio Victoria, Robin Wood, Sydney Humphreys, and James Hunter (standing), 1989. (Victoria Conservatory of Music)

Glynis Leyshon and the Belfrey Theatre, 1981. (Ian McKain, Victoria *Times-Colonist*)

Pianist Gertrude Huntly Green (1889–1987) in 1927. (G. H.

Stanley Shale (1899–1968), Victoria's master music teacher (E.M. Johnson)

Hans Gruber, conductor of t toria Symphony Orchestra 63. (Victoria *Times-Colonist*

a–vi

Production of *I Remember Mama*, directed by Audrey Johnson for the Victoria Theatre Guild, October 1950, showing (l. to r.) Henry Stubbings, Noel Cusack (standing), May Hulholland (seated), Annabelle Keane (kneeling), Allan Keyworth (seated), Janet Bartholomew (kneeling), John Keane (seated), and Diana Ricardo (on steps). (Victoria Theatre Guild)

The Langham Court Theatre at 805 Langham Court in 1959 (City of Victoria Archives)

Noel Cusack in *The Barretts of Wimpole Street*, June 1949. (Noel Cusack)

Helen Smith, winner of the Best Actress Award in the bc Drama Festival, January 1951, in *The Heiress*. (Duncan Macphail)

Ada (Mrs. J. F. K.) English, matriarch of the Greater Victoria Music Festival, May 1981. (Bill Halkett, Victoria *Times-Colonist*)

Peter Mannering, founder of the Bastion Theatre, July 1973. (Victoria *Times-Colonist*)

Anthony Jenkins and Marge Bridgeman in *Butley* at the Victoria Theatre Guild, March, 1985. (Hans F. Dietrich, Victoria *Times-Colonist*)

Graham Steed, Organist and Choirmaster at Christ Church Cathedral 1949–58. (Jim Ryan, Victoria *Times-Colonist*)

Sam Payne and Marjorie LeStrange in Bastion Theatre's performance of *Five Finger Exercise*, 1971. (Ian McKain, University of Victoria Archives)

Peter Brockington with Irena Mayeska in Bastion Theatre's production of *Richard III*, February, 1977. (Barry Casson, University of Victoria Archives)

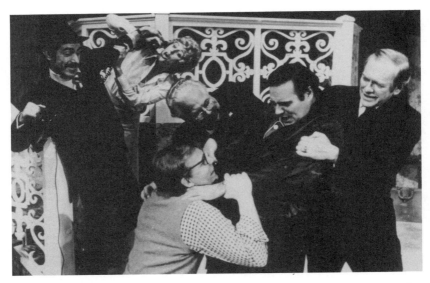

Bastion Theatre's production of *Born Yesterday*, 1974, showing Peter Mannering (back centre) with Al Kozlik, Nonnie Griffin, Michael Ball, Owen Foran, and Vernon Chapman. (Ian McKain, University of Victoria Archives)

Bastion Theatre's production of *Deathtrap*, February 1980, with Douglas Rain and Myra Benson. (University of Victoria Archives)

Bastion Theatre's production of *Life with Father*, December 1979, showing the young Andrew Sabiston (back r.) in his first major role. (University of Victoria Archives)

Bastion Youth Touring Company performs *Androcles the Lion and Friends*, 1979. Pictured are Jayne Healey and Roy Vine. (Bastion Theatre)

On the set of *Jitters* (April 1980), declaring Bastion Theatre Month, we see (l. to r.) Mayor Bill Tindall , Hugh Henderson, Michael Field, Maryla Waters, Clare Copeland, and Edwin Stephenson (standing). (Bastion Theatre)

CHAPTER EIGHT

Music Festivals

HILE Victoria musicians had been competing in the British Columbia Music Festival in Vancouver since its inception in 1923 it was not until 1927 that Victoria had a competitive music festival of its own. The first sessions were held on 21–23 April with about 400 entries in 40 classes. While other Canadian festivals of the period (of which there were a considerable number) subscribed to the British "chain" of adjudicators who were hired to service one festival after another across the country, Victoria hired its own. These included Dr. Edward Broome of Calgary (choral and vocal), Carl Denton of Portland (piano and violin), Percy Campbell of Portland (piano and violin), Graham Morgan of Seattle (choral and vocal), and Nellie Cornish, founder of the famous Cornish School of Seattle (elocution).

By 1931 the event was advertised as the "International Festival of the Northwest" due to the extensive participation of competitors from Washington and Oregon. In that year the British chain was used for the first time. The British adjudicators had plenty of informative and even inspiring things to say. There was much to be learned and the sessions could be of prime educational value, but the showmanship of the adjudicators transcended, at times, their eagerness to teach. As with most instinctive performers, witticisms spilled over in response to audience reaction, sometimes to the verge of cruelty.

A typical and unforgettable example concerned a young woman vocalist in a B grade class singing Dvořák's *Songs My Mother Taught Me* with its characteristic swooping glissandi. The adjudicator commented that the performer reminded him of the jest about the person who had travelled across the Atlantic "by rail"! The shout of laughter from the audience may have flattered the adjudicator's flair for entertainment but it certainly could have done little for the competitor. This competition festival was loaded down with silver medals, shields, and other trophies and almost nothing in the way of useful cash awards.

Participation in the festival reached a high of 831 competitors in 1935 but fell to a low of 661 in 1939. This, coupled with the difficulty of engaging British adjudicators because of the war and a general lack of attendance at all sessions, caused a "temporary" suspension of operations.

It was with the coming of Ada and J. F. K. English (who had had wide festival experience in Kamloops) and Mary and Roberto Wood (who had close connections with the Winnipeg festival movement) that the bricks of a new Victoria music festival began to fall into place. Because of a series of columns I had written on the subject I was invited by Dr. English to attend a meeting in 1947 to discuss re-establishing the music festival. This historic meeting was held at Craigdarroch Castle which, at that time, housed the School Board offices.

Among other important decisions made was the consensus to do away with the former festival's dozens of trophies and medals, all of which had been meticulously hoarded in someone's basement or attic. Mutely, I gave thanks, remembering that the former festival had become an obvious and often ridiculous pot-hunt. The exceptions to this were that the BC Electric Rose Bowl was to be awarded to the top vocal entrant in the "open" class and that the City of Victoria Medallion (which, in fact, is a large silver tray) was to be awarded to the top piano entrant in the "open" class. One or two of the former school trophies were also retained. The older trophies, according to Ada English, were gathered together and taken to a jeweller where they were melted down, and the resulting funds from the considerable quantity of tarnished silver were used to create a scholarship.

Another major, and practical, decision involved rewarding outstanding performances with bursaries and scholarships, many of which are donated by individuals, organizations, and businesses. A number of bursary awards were also to be provided from the proceeds of ticket and programme sales. Some awards were eventually offered as memorials and included the Dr. J. F. K. English Memorial Award, the McPherson Foundation "Most Distinguished Performer" Award, and a scholarship established by the Woods "for continued learning and development in music." The first competitions of the new Greater Victoria Music Festival were held in May 1950 with more than 600 competitors.

When asked about competition at festivals, Ada stated: "I think competition is healthy, provided it is approached in the right way and providing the teacher and parents don't get involved in the sense of it becoming a confrontation. Youngsters themselves don't seem to mind. Competition is quite natural to children. They usually don't get upset if someone else wins. Of course they enjoy winning . . . but when parents lay great emphasis on how a child placed — 'you could have come first if you'd done more work' — that's when pressure starts and pleasure begins to disappear. I think our festival is enjoying the happy medium where we have both competitive and non-competitive classes. We try to impress on entrants that what they have received is one person's opinion formed in one interval of time. Another adjudicator might see things differently."

On 10 April 1981 Fred English died suddenly while on an errand for the approaching festival. Everyone involved in the festival's many aspects deeply felt the loss of this remarkable man. True to the standards of both husband and wife and in spite of her loss, Ada English remained at her secretarial post in the festival office during the entire three-week run of that 1981 Festival "because," she stated, "Fred would have wanted it that way."

I once asked Ada if she had a pet peeve or two. Her answer: "Yes, I do. Top of my list would be people who don't bother reading what has been printed in the syllabus, the programs, the newspaper, on posters and signs. So many of the telephone calls we get in the Festival office — and we get dozens — are complaints and questions that would be unnecessary if people read what was written."

Ada remained a staunch supporter and willing worker in the festival movement until her death on 18 February 1994.

The Greater Victoria Music Festival has had a profound influence upon the lives of many students. Ada mentions specifically the Abbotts — Jocelyn, Vivian, and Norman — as well as Walter Prossnitz, Richard Margison, Alan Reiser, May-Ling Kwok, and Lynn Hendry from the early years of the revived festival as well as Bob Tweten, Monica Pfau, Michelle Himmick, and Cary Chow from the 1980s.

The Victoria Festival's impressive growth from a one-week event in 1949 to a full month of sessions is due to many factors. Perhaps the most important of these include the de-emphasis on competition, the awarding of bursaries and scholarships as opposed to trophies, and adjudications that are more in the nature of creative teacher-talk based on helpful assistance rather than a surgical "picking apart" that inevitably leaves raw ends — a situation I often witnessed in prewar festivals.

The Victoria International Festival, a "festival" in the true sense of the word, began in the 1970s in association with J. J. Johannesen's International School of the Arts. The school was originally conceived as a high-quality international summer training centre "dedicated towards advanced and talented music students who have already decided to make music their career or who wish to advance their recently launched career." The training centre, a BC Centennial project, originated at the Shawnigan Lake School in 1971 and moved to St. Michael's University School in Victoria in 1974. Johannesen's objective was to attract outstanding teachers of voice and various instruments who would offer private tuition and master classes to enrolled students in addition to giving public performances as part of the International Festival.

Though the school came first, it was inevitable that public concerts should develop through the presence of outstanding performer-teachers. Initially these were put together on a spur-of-the-moment basis, but following the move to Victoria the full-scale festival that we enjoy today quickly blossomed. A goal of the school is to "hire outstanding faculty of world-renowned artists who desire to pass on the wealth of their success and experience to a new generation." Outstanding instrumental teachers who have both taught and performed for the Johannesen school/festival include Canadians Robert Aitken, James Campbell, Taras Gabora, Robin McCabe, Gary Karr, and Gerald Stanick, in addition to many teachers from the U.S. and abroad. A chamber music course with the Orford String Quartet in residence was begun in 1975 and an electronic music course was introduced in 1978.

The initial purpose of the festival was to provide the students attending the school with exposure to the teacher-artist through live public concerts. Eventually, the festival grew through overwhelming response from the Victoria public to become, as well, a tourist attraction bringing people from all over Canada. The six-week-long event normally features some 30 concerts.

In 1978 an opera centre was introduced with both students and faculty involved in chamber opera productions under the title Canada Opera Piccola. Originators of the programme were the husband and wife team of Léopold Simoneau and Pierrette Alarie, while other teacher-performers included Gaelyne Gabora and Phyllis Mailing. The programme limited its enrolment to 12 students (in order to maintain a healthy student-to-teacher ratio), and auditions to enter the programme were held right across Canada. The students chosen receive free tuition and a weekly stipend of $200 for rent and food. The faculty expected that all students come with decent training and that they considered the school as the necessary step between study and the professional stage. Simoneau was in charge of all the vocal work for the operas while Alarie handled the staging. One of the operas prepared in the summer was sometimes toured across Canada and into the US in the fall. On the tour students were paid equity rates plus an expense allotment. While an orchestra was employed for the tour the first season, this was found to be too expensive and piano accompaniment only was used later. Canada Opera Piccola disappeared, unfortunately, from the Festival in the early 1990s.

Over the years, the Victoria International Festival has brought outstanding artists to Victoria who have provided hundreds of musical events to an otherwise barren summer musical season. While Johannesen died in 1994, because of the tight organizational structure which he had established, there is every indication that both the school and the festival will carry on for many years to come.

The link between music and theatre provides the ultimate experience in the performing arts, and in this area, too, Victoria has excelled.

CHAPTER NINE

Music Theatre and
Pacific Opera Victoria

M Y first memories of locally-produced music theatre were performances by the Victoria Civic Opera directed by Basil Horsfall. Horsfall who had retired to Cobble Hill after a wide international experience in opera and the film arts, beginning as musical director of the Carl Rosa Opera Company based in London, England. It was during a tour of that company that Basil met his wife, Elfrida, who would later become a vocal coach of some significance and his lifelong companion in opera production. The Horsfalls emigrated to the US in 1912 and came to Montreal in 1917 where he was involved in the film industry and directed opera productions. He spent much time on the west coast and produced one of the first opera films, *The Bohemian Girl*, in Vancouver in 1923, involving live opera singers on stage with the film.

Disenchanted with quiet pastoral life on the island, the Horsfalls soon became involved with the musical life of Victoria and began working with the remaining members of the old Victoria Operatic Society (no relation to the present organization of the same name) under the title Victoria Philharmonic Society. This later became the Victoria Civic Opera and, in 1937, the Victoria Grand Opera Association. Horsfall considered these companies essentially as training grounds for potential operatic singers and began with concert productions (no stage action) of *Il Trovatore* and *Faust*. In 1935 the new Civic Opera produced their first full-scale production, Wagner's *Lohengrin*.

The only thing I can clearly recall about that sally into the grand opera field is that the only available tenor who could aspire to

Wagnerian roles came over from Seattle. He had a well-trained voice, if not ideally Wagnerian, but moved stiffly because of the unfortunate factor of an artificial leg.[1] As a result the poor man had a dreadful struggle getting in and out of Lohengrin's rather wobbly swan boat. Like so many other moments in history the productions of these companies were over-weighted by ambition but not altogether without merit. Some of the solo voices and the experienced conducting were particularly noteworthy. Critics felt that the company had "over-reached" itself in attempting so difficult a work for their first production and it was obvious that the company and its directors felt similarly, for their next two shows were the much lighter *The Chocolate Soldier* (1935) and *The Bandit Princess* (1936).

The latter work was an original operetta composed by Horsfall on a libretto by Canadian writer W. A. Tremayne. Horsfall had written several operas before, including *Cartita*, *Cleopatra* (which ran for 65 performances in the US), and *Queen of the Fair*, but the composer acknowledged that *The Bandit Princess* was by far his best. The critics agreed, likening his score to the mature works of Victor Herbert and others of that period, and calling his melodies "tuneful and catchy."

The establishment of Horsfall's Grand Opera Association in 1936 marked a swing back to the educational function in which both he and his wife so firmly believed. Most of the works produced over the next six years would be mounted for small audiences at the Association's clubrooms at 1753 Rockland (one of Victoria's larger mansions) and sometimes consisted of only single acts from the standard repertoire produced with minimal lighting, stage sets, and

---

1 Audrey is actually referring here to Carl Horthy (born Douglas C. Horth) who was, in fact, a native of Victoria. He played Lohengrin for the Victoria Civic Opera on 18–19 October, 1935 at the Royal Victoria Theatre and was likely living here at the time. He had lost his leg at Ypres during the First World War. He later moved to Toronto where he established a relatively successful career despite his incapacitation. He died there on 18 September 1964 , at the age of 71. (ed.)

costumes. These productions lasted until 1942 and were designed, essentially, to give the young singers experience on the stage.

In 1940 Horsfall began a collaboration with E. V. Young for a summer series of musical dramas at Malkin Bowl in Stanley Park in Vancouver. This move would become Theatre Under the Stars (TUTS), one of Western Canada's most significant summer festivals. In its early years Horsfall drew heavily upon singers he had trained in the Victoria Grand Opera Association to fill major roles in TUTS productions. These included Fraser Lister, David Oldham, James McVie, and Thelma Johns, among others. Horsfall moved to Vancouver after Elfrida's death in 1943 and he died there in 1950 while conducting a rehearsal for his favourite opera, *Carmen*. A link between Victoria and TUTS was the establishment in 1948 of the Victoria Theatre Foundation which remounted TUTS productions under the name Starlight Theatre at Royal Athletic Park and then later, due to a season of inclement weather, at Memorial Arena.

In 1945 a small group of young women, all members of Christ Church Cathedral choir, put their heads together and decided to form a Gilbert and Sullivan society with the intent of mounting major items of that repertoire. Their names were Barbara (Gurney) Stark, Jean (Harness) Haddaway, Norah Hughes, Gwynedd Hughes, Bunny (Hughes) Cowan, and Pamela (Terry) Beckwith. They progressed with this idea, established an executive committee, and acquired the enthusiastic cooperation of Melvin Knudsen as their musical director. They opened at the Royal on 24 June 1946 with what is perhaps the simplest of these absurd, melodious, and adored classics of the operetta stage, *HMS Pinafore*. Its success was instantaneous and the whole concept was soundly endorsed by audiences and press. The Society continued to offer Gilbert and Sullivan repertoire for several seasons until they — and likewise their audiences — began to tire of repetition and it was agreed to turn to New York for twentieth-century choices. They continued to do good work including an occasional Gilbert and Sullivan revival while audiences remained faithful and growing.

There came a day, however, that a name change seemed appropriate when there appeared to be no indication that they would return to the Gilbert and Sullivan repertoire. They chose the title Victoria Operatic Society and have continued to do two musicals each year, drawing near capacity houses for a week's run at the McPherson Playhouse. Their presentations have ranged all the way from the once popular Victor Herbert and Romberg works to those of Rogers and Hammerstein, Lerner and Loewe, George Gershwin, and Stephen Sondheim. This venture stands alongside the striking success of the Victoria Theatre Guild as acknowledging the steady contribution to a city's culture that can be made by inspired amateurs.

The Victoria Theatre Guild also moved into the production of musicals on occasion and, in fact, operated the Victoria Little Theatre Orchestra in the 1930s to provide musical accompaniment for many of their shows. In 1947 Winifred Lugrin Fahey, a local singer who had had success in both Eastern Canada and New York, formed the Victoria Light Opera Company as a vehicle for the presentation of her own compositions. She joined forces with the Victoria Theatre Guild and mounted her first production, *The Bride Ship*, at the Little Theatre in October, 1947. The most popular of Fahey's creations, it is based upon the true story arrival of the famous *Tynemouth* in Victoria Harbour in April 1862 with a number of marriageable young ladies on board, each destined (at least in the magical world of musical comedy) to find a husband. *The Bride Ship* was revived in 1957 and remounted in 1958 and 1965. It was also produced at Guelph, Galt, and twice in Toronto in the 1950s. By the time of her second production, *The Spirit of the Nile* (1948) Fahey had severed her relationship with the Guild (by mutual agreement, I understand) and had struck out on her own. Further performances of this group included *Paris Rendezvous* (1949), *And So, Her Ladyship* (1950) and *The Jewel of Loodipoor* (1950 and 1959) all written by Fahey.

My first experience with opera from the director's chair was a production of *Yeomen of the Guard* for the Gilbert and Sullivan Society in May, 1958. The success of this production led to a second request from the Society, this time to help them mount their first

offer them." The choir was understandably apprehensive about the need to move rhythmically up the aisles of the cathedral while singing, for few had any experience in stage musicals. The solution was to have the choir sing off-stage in the shadows of the ambulatory while the shepherds and shepherdesses acting the scene were recruited mainly from the Victoria Theatre Guild.

The first *Amahl* done in a Canadian cathedral turned out to be an unqualified success. Each of the four performances had overflow audiences and the funds collected were sufficient to provide a nest egg for a projected second production. People were asking Dean Whitlow if it would be done again the following Christmas; was it to become an annual event? The Dean talked it over with me and made his point that, delightful and successful though it was, it did put extra strain on the cathedral staff. He didn't think it would be fair to them or to me and Maurice to attempt it every Christmas. I agreed and then he suggested that we should plan to do it every third Christmas, thus establishing a tradition for a short time.

We repeated *Amahl* six times at the Cathedral between 1959 and 1974 and had only one financial failure. That was in 1968 when, on leaving Christ Church after our habitual Boxing Day dress rehearsal, we found that snow had fallen to a depth of nearly eight inches. It did not disappear overnight, either, but hung around with freezing temperatures for the better part of a week. In Victoria this meant no audiences to speak of and a financial loss for the cathedral. *Amahl* was allowed to rest awhile after that frustrating episode but at Dean Whitlow's invitation it was revived once more in 1978.

A decade later, after I retired from the *Times-Colonist*, Frances Pollet, founding-director of the award-winning Linden Singers and music director for St. Matthias Church at the time, asked Maurice and me if we could meet with her to discuss the logistics of producing *Amahl* in the church hall for the Christmas season of 1988. At that meeting we described the process we went through to mount the opera successfully so many times.

What I had perceived in the first presentation of Amahl was the clear simplicity of the story: the widowed mother, scarcely able to feed her crippled child who, forgetting hunger in his wonder at the great star seeming to float above their croft, begs her in vain to come and see. Then follows the arrival of the three Kings and their slave, seeking a few hours' rest. Kaspar's parrot fascinates Amahl but the mother's eyes are all for the chest of gold. She wonders if the Kings would miss it if she took just a little for her child's sake. She creeps over to the chest and slips her hand in, clutching a few gold pieces. The slave awakes, seizes her, and calls out that she is a thief. There is a struggle in which Amahl tries to defend his mother. The Kings rise and Melchior tells her, "Woman, you may keep the gold. The King we seek does not need our gold…" and continues to describe the Christ Child who will be born that night.

The mother says: "No, no. Take back your gold. If I were not so poor I would bring a gift of my own to such a child."

This is where the miracle must take place. If it doesn't work, the whole meaning and climax of this small operatic gem is lost. Greatly moved, Amahl cries out, "But mother, let me send him my crutch, for this I made myself, and who knows he may need one!" and he starts forward extending the crutch toward the kings in his two hands, moving several paces as his mother cries, "You can't … you can't." Amahl places the crutch in the King's hand and moves back with a few tentative steps crying out over and over, "I walk, Mother! … I walk, Mother!"

To succeed without blemish in its poignant climax it cannot — indeed must not — seem contrived, or else all its impulse and spirituality is lost. The director and Amahl may often have to work together for several hours during the formative stages of rehearsal to break down the self-consciousness that can destroy the ultimate effect.

After my short homily there was silence. Then we were asked if we might attend certain initial phases of rehearsal — just to make sure they were on the right track. Maurice and I looked at each other and then I said "would you like us to take it on?" The answer was an immediate and unqualified "yes!"

So we went to work once again with an enthusiastic cast that included soprano Judith Dowling as the Mother and promising musician Philip Bowers as Amahl and an eager-spirited crew. I know that neither of us ever enjoyed the undertaking more. Unfortunately I had to leave them just before dress rehearsal to enter hospital. Sydney Sparling, who had perfectly understood and choreographed the shepherds' dance sequence, together with stage manager Jean Topham and Maurice were able to see it through its last phase of staging. David Watson was the pianist and a pleasing addition was the oboe played by Anne Moyls.

The fact that Victoria's Christ Church was the first to present the poignant little gem in a Canadian cathedral was due largely to Dean Whitlow's desire to have theatre reunited with the church whence had come drama's origin. These are experiences, spiritually and artistically, that I shall never forget.

In the early 1960s the Musical Art Society became interested in the production of operatic works as a vehicle to challenge the many young singers then being trained in Victoria. I was approached by the executive of the Society to assist them in mounting works of substance which would enrich the then barren operatic field. This led to two productions, Purcell's *Dido and Æneas* (January, 1961) and Puccini's *Gianni Schicchi* (May, 1962), being mounted in the Oak Bay High School auditorium. These involved many of Victoria's best young singers, including Peggy Walton Packard, Adele Goult-Lewis, Anne Harris, June Milburn-Gruber, Margaret Abbott, Marguerite Hobbs, Norman Tyrrell, Hans Steffan, John "Jock" Dunbar, and the incomparable Linc Painter, among others.

The connection with Christ Church Cathedral initiated by the productions of *Amahl and the Night Vistors* led to the mounting of two dramatic pieces in that noble edifice, T. S. Eliot's *Murder in the Cathedral* in November, 1966, and Peter Luke's *Hadrian the Seventh* in February, 1973. It was only through the complete cooperation and encouragment of the Cathedral's Chapter and staff, especially Dean Brian Whitlow, that these productions were possible at all. It was because of the significance of these works coupled with the venue where they were presented that resulted in our ability to attract the best of Victoria's amateur and professional actors to participate.

Memorable among these performances were Gerald Webb as Thomas Beckett and John Heath as Fr. William Rolfe (later Hadrian VII). Other local thespians involved included Jack Droy, Allan Purdy, John Drean, Richard Litt, Sheila Litt, John Britt, Ron Way, Michæl Meiklejohn, Barry Grimshaw, and John Goult.

Music theatre from 1945 to the 1990s was dominated largely by productions of the Victoria Operatic Society (vos). With little support from government grants or sponsors and no reduction on the rental of the McPherson Playhouse, where they have produce their shows since 1965, the Society is dependent solely on their audiences for financial support. A typical show costs between $70,000 and $80,000 to produce with 70% of this going to royalties, theatre rentals, and the cost of professional musicians. A theatre capacity of 75% is necessary for the group to "break even" but over the years they have maintained a steady following of patrons which often sell out their performances well in advance of opening night. The society, which currently has a membership of about 200, is fortunate in owning their own rehearsal hall and set-construction facility and all labour is volunteer, keeping costs to a minimum.

In the fall of 1978 the executive, under the guiding hand of president Ron Webb, purchased a warehouse in Esquimalt in which sets would be built and costumes and props stored. The facility was named "Massam Hall" in memory of George Massam who, for many years, was responsible for the beautiful sets seen on stage. In the spring of 1983 the adjoining building was purchased and converted to the sets facility while the other building was renovated during the summer months to include a kitchen, board room, and a rehearsal hall designed to the dimensions of the McPherson stage. The new facility, named Hughes Hall after the Hughes sisters, also includes larger costume storage and a make-up workshop.

Perhaps the most ambitious of the vos productions was the light opera *Die Fledermaus*, first mounted in 1959 and revived in 1977. The first production was described by the critics as "an outstanding production by amateurs that reached professional heights." The second production, however, fell short of this mark, lacking a concept of the style of the period and full of clichés but empty of humour and interesting business. *My Fair Lady* (1978), on the other hand, clearly showed the director had an understanding of the nature, and style of the show, resulting in performances which were clearly outstanding.

Oklahoma! has been, perhaps, the most popular of the VOS shows and was mounted four times, in 1959 (radio), 1966, 1975, and 1989. The performance of 1975 penetrated about as far into the realm of professionalism as an amateur society is likely to go. Directed by Allan Purdy with Tudor Jones on the podium the cast presented a lively and well-paced show. Another success and in an idiom which the VOS does not often explore was *Jesus Christ, Superstar,* first mounted in 1979. *The Best Little Whorehouse in Texas* (1987) made great demands on the dancing ability of its members and was thoroughly enjoyed by those who did not find its subject matter too risqué for conservative Victoria.

By the time of the Society's 40th anniversary in 1985 they had produced 74 shows and celebrated that occasion with their fourth mounting of Gilbert and Sullivan's *The Mikado* on the 100th anniversary of its first production. It is to be particularly noted that local high school teacher Howard Denike was musical director for more than 20 of the VOS shows beginning in 1965.

On occasion, the Society has combined forces with other local organizations to produce special entertainments. The first of these ventures was *Duo* (1961) when the Victoria Theatre Guild produced the one-act play *Family Album* while the VOS presented *Trial By Jury* in the second half. "Our aim," according to Janet Senior, "was to get 'Playgoers' to see a musical and 'musicalgoers' to see a play." Another successful experiment involved the mounting of four musicals for radio presentation on CJVI, *The Bohemian Girl* (1958), *Oklahoma!* (1959), *Carousel* (1963), and *Show Boat* (1964).

Meanwhile, at the Victoria Conservatory of Music, voice department head Catherine Young was setting the stage for the creation of Victoria's first professional opera company, Pacific Opera Victoria. The Conservatory's first tentative presentations of opera were small-scale events, both cost and experience being limiting factors. Assuming the title "Opera in Action" in 1971 and with Catherine Young as artistic director they mounted a performance of *The Magic Flute* in concert form at the MacLaurin Auditorium (now the David Lam Auditorium) at UVIC. Still using the "concert" format they carried forward with performances of *Orpheus in the Underworld* and *The Marriage of Figaro* in 1973 and, in the spring of 1974, *Don Giovanni* was presented at the McPherson Playhouse. Since these included no stage action to distract the singers, all performances were positively embraced by the audiences and the critics.

Due to the musical and financial success of these early efforts, the group assumed the title Vancouver Island Opera Society (later shortened to VanIsle Opera) in 1976 and took a long step forward with a fully staged production of Mozart's *The Marriage of Figaro*. Seattle conductor Stanley Chapple was invited as musical director and the Victoria Symphony was in the pit. Well received, it owed much to a professionally-oriented ensemble including the late Ruth Champion as the Countess, Garth Gislason as Count Almaviva, Dawn Hood as Cherubino, Judy Temple as Susanna, Selena James as Marcellina, and Charles Dorrington as an assured Figaro. Winning positive audience acceptance, it had many pleasant and even enchanting moments. This success, unfortunately, encouraged a longer step taken too soon.

For a second presentation, *The Magic Flute* was selected for the fall of 1977. Sets and costumes on an Egyptian theme were by Carole Sabiston, the stage director was Colin Skinner, and Stanley Chapple was again at the podium. This work proved almost impossible to cast appropriately and its complexity of staging suffered, predominantly due to budget restrictions. Due to the short time frame the group allowed themselves, under-rehearsal was the first element that one was acutely aware of on opening night. Despite the attitude that "we should only be judged as amateurs," note was taken of this and other negative criticism which resulted in the company selecting lighter works for its next ventures, John Gay's *The Beggar's*

Opera (which is hardly an opera at all) and Smetana's *The Bartered Bride* (1978). These sat much more comfortably with the potential of the company, although no one among the audiences could have suspected that they were witnessing the birth of an organization that was to become one of the most successful professional operatic companies in Canada. VanIsle Opera continued with Christmas performances of *Amahl and the Night Visitors* and *Cinderella* until the tide changed in 1980 with the beginnings of Pacific Opera Victoria (the "Victoria" was added later to avoid confusion about its base of operations).

Grand opera has always been considered to be an élitist art form in smaller cities such as Victoria and therefore only able to attract minority audiences. What began here as an extension of the Conservatory of Music's vocal department has developed into a separate and fully professional company that is firmly rooted in the city. It is noted throughout Canada's musical fraternity and is sailing an even course financially thanks largely to the astute fund-raising capabilities of its past-president, George Heffelfinger, and his wife, Jane. In addition to an inspired board, while essential to success, little could be achieved without the operatic flair and solid musical background of artistic director Timothy Vernon, who adds to his technical competence and scholarship an exceptional and natural flair for the dramatic.

Stage directors of operatic productions are frequently the last persons mentioned in a review and are lucky if they are granted a couple of lines. Only the company, the music director, and those few among audiences who have experienced the demanding job are likely to be capable of appraising this aspect of a production. Similarly, a set designer's concept may be lovely to look at and delight the audience but still not work well for the actors, as we have already seen, and vice versa. On the whole, however, Pacific Opera has been consistently well served — who could forget *Abduction from the Seraglio* (1981), *Tosca* (1983), and *Il Trovatore* (1986), for example — by its designers and its stage directors. Glynis Leyshon, who would later become artistic director for the Belfry Theatre, is particularly remembered for her innovative approach to *The Barber of Seville* (1980) and *Abduction from the Seraglio.*

Other often unsung heroes in opera production are the costume and set designers. Particularly memorable in this area were the costumes of Carole Sabiston and the sets of Bill West for the 1981 production of *Madama Butterfly*. Pacific Opera has a singular advantage (although some might call it a disadvantage) in that the stage of the McPherson Playhouse is, according to Jane Heffelfinger, "the size of a postage stamp." Thus scenic designers have to be hired and all sets must be created "from scratch" instead of being rented from Vancouver, Seattle, or San Francisco. The advantage here is the opportunity this gives both the director and the designer to create new insights and not be bound by tradition. Pacific Opera has gained the reputation over the years for doing things in an innovative and creative way and this has resulted in people coming from all down the west coast to see "how it is done in Victoria." Some of these, especially from Vancouver and Seattle, are subscribers and a few are even donors.

A particularly memorable experience of innovative simplicity for me was the collective indrawn breath of the audience as the curtain rose on Jack Simon's setting for Selim's palace in *Abduction*. This was a beautifully proportioned set design that from its basic modules altered, smoothly and efficiently, three times, each change richly satisfying in every detail.

Opportunities for creative designing also are found in the costume department, with the 1984 production of *Carmen*, for instance, being done in modern dress. The director, Christopher Newton, tended to pull the designers and the singers out and the result was a wonderful, savage piece of work that was so stark, so strong, and so powerful that you thought it was being created for the first time. Not all operas can benefit from the kind of approach that Newton took, but *Carmen* is concerned with passions that are still completely with us today and it really worked in this instance. Kay Frick of the Metropolitan Opera in New York and her husband, Richard (who produces the Metropolitan Opera broadcasts), saw Pacific Opera's *Carmen* and she is quoted as stating that she had never seen a *Carmen* she enjoyed so much because it was so intimate and so meaningful to today's world.

Another unique advantage that Pacific Opera has is its ability (in fact, the necessity) to play in a small, intimate house. Most opera companies are forced to play to two or three thousand people per performance. Here they are able to give an opera experience that is a true reflection of the European experience of two or three hundred years ago.

Because of its limited budget and also due to its innovative approach, Pacific Opera can attract many rising young singers who need that first experience with their role before moving on to the bigger houses. Phillip Enns, for instance, did his first Figaro here and then moved on to recreate the same role in Edmonton, Calgary, Winnipeg, and New York. Similarly, Kathleen Brett did her first Juliet with Pacific Opera, Vincent Cole sang his first Pinkerton, and Paul Frey did his first Tosca here. The other side of that coin is the fact that more mature singers often appreciate an opportunity to rework an old role. They want to take a fresh approach to reinterpreting it in a less exposed environment where they can take risks. Pacific Opera is often that "less exposed environment" and there have been some exciting and notable experiences as singers feel that here they can sing "on the edge" and not end up ruining their careers.

In the summer of 1984 a summer festival was attempted by Pacific Opera with a production of *The Merry Widow*. Eight performances were planned as opposed to the normal five and all were well attended but, with such a small staff, there was insufficient time to do proper planning between this and the spring production of *Carmen*. While the experiment was, in many ways, successful, there were not sufficient resources to sustain or market it and the concept was abandoned.

A coup for the company was achieved when the 1985 board of directors decided to introduce the scheme of "surtitles" (translations) projected above the proscenium in the McPherson Playhouse.

This was definitely a better solution to audience complaints of "not understanding what was being said" than the more common one — that of singing an English translation of the text. Such translations are generally awkward and less musically compatible than the original language as far as the singers are concerned. While the director of the Vancouver Opera once commented that he had no intention of following the surtitle route, the Queen Elizabeth Theatre now displays this text when opera in its original language has the stage.

Under the musical direction of resident maestro Timothy Vernon there is no quarrel with tempi and accuracy of style in any production. As for the imperfect balance between orchestra and singers (the single most frequently heard criticism among opera-goers), the fault lies primarily with the absence of anything that can factually be described as an "orchestra pit" in the McPherson Playhouse. As the century enters its last decade the Royal Theatre also, despite handsome and costly improvements to front-of-house, continues to lack an adequate orchestra pit and has backstage problems.

Pacific Opera is currently healthy if not exactly wealthy. While the size of the the McPherson has many advantages, it has certain disadvantages. Subscriptions to the series have been increasing every year. In 1989-90 they were up 43% and in 1990-91 increased by another 52%. Between subscriptions and first single-ticket buyers all good seats are gone well before opening night. The 1989 production of *Eugene Onegin* — not the most popular of all operas — was sold out for all performances and it was impossible to get tickets for *Der Freischütz* (1993) after opening night.

In an attempt to solve this problem the 1992 production of *Die Fledermaus* was moved to the larger Royal Theatre and in 1993 *The Merry Widow* was similarly mounted at the Royal. While the intimacy of the McPherson is lost in these moves, a three-night run at the Royal can generate the almost same income as a six-night run at the McPherson with fewer expenses. Sponsorship by such foundations and business as Du Maurier Arts, Shell, PetroCanada, and the Royal Bank have helped to keep ticket prices down while still retaining the intimacy of the McPherson. If these subsidies are lost, rising costs dictate that a total move to the Royal seems inevitable.

As the century draws to a close, Pacific Opera has become firmly established and is widely known for its quality productions. Like the Victoria Symphony, it has become a hot box-office property. Its success is due not only to astute management, but also to the support of a far-sighted board.

It is the area of pure theatre, however, that has engaged the imagination and talents of more Victorians than any other of the performing arts.

CHAPTER TEN

Curtains Rose and Fell

A T the time when the Great Depression was spreading over North America, there was one man in Victoria who brought fresh life into British Columbia's scattered regional theatre activity. He was to make his knowledge and passion for theatre into a lifeline, at least for the morale of hundreds of people on the island and all over the province who desperately needed diversion from the constant cycle of purposeless days and weeks.

The man who was to provide that diversion was Llewellyn Bullock-Webster, popularly known as Bill or "the Major." He was a product of the professional theatre in Britain and had had distinguished service in the First World War during which he had risen to the rank of Major. He had emigrated to BC and lived for a time in Prince Rupert where his dynamic energy and unmistakable gift of leadership earned him a seat on the city council.

He had always nurtured a dream, however, to launch and run a drama school. Examining his situation he realized that its chances of success would be better in a larger city. So he moved with his wife and young son to the capital. There, having obtained the patronage and support of some of Victoria's wealthy and arts-conscious citizens, he established his British Columbia Dramatic School. It was located on the upper floor of one of the two-storey buildings (still extant) on the south side of Fort Street between Douglas and Broad. He also conducted drama classes on a weekly basis on the mainland at the Hotel Vancouver.

Occasionally the Major brought noted personalities in the literary as well as the theatre world to talk to his students and guests. Although my later life was to involve me profoundly with theatre as a hobby and ultimately as a journalist, my first and only visit to the British Columbia Dramatic School was on the occasion of a guest appearance by the Baroness Orczy. She was at that time creator of the heroic Scarlet Pimpernel. My mother welcomed the chance to see, and possibly meet, the author and took me along. In the end, even to my juvenile mind, Orczy was quite upstaged by the Major who dominated the show with all the skills of a to-the-manor-born ringmaster. I distinctly recall the incident and that Orczy was predictably theatrical in apparel but relatively uninspiring in presentation.

Things had been developing reasonably well for the British Columbia Dramatic School until the economic effects of Depression began to be felt. Students disappeared as parents suffered income losses and soon Bill had to close his school. It took him from his position among the town's cultural élite to join the throngs seeking whatever job might be available and for a time he worked as an assistant gardener at the Empress Hotel. Never one to be "put down," the Major soon became Victoria Secretary for the CPR Music Department which involved organizing the cultural programming for the Empress Hotel. One of the features that Bill developed was the now internationally known Elizabethan Christmas Festival. Bill's experience had taught him what powerful therapy was to be found in theatre activity. As he raked leaves and hoed weeds he kept thinking that if people could only be involved in some time-consuming distraction, such as amateur theatre, it would help them survive the bad times. He wondered if there was a way that such activity on a wide basis could be brought about. Ever thinking positively and on a broad scale, he devised a plan for the development of amateur drama across the entire province.

When it was complete he took the proposition to Dr. G. M. Weir, then Minister of Education. His proposal included government sponsorship in organizing theatre groups in the communities most affected by the sag in the economy. These groups would be given help and direction. Each spring, festivals would be organized in the various districts and winners from each district would then be brought to Victoria in May to compete in the week-long British Columbia Drama Festival. Bill further conceived the idea of a Western Canada Theatre Conference to be held at the final weekend. This would include talks on various aspects of theatre as therapy and how best to achieve satisfactory results in addition to exchanges of ideas and question-and-answer sessions.

His enthusiasm and positive approach, together with the government's anxiety to be seen to provide some sort of anodyne for the stressed population, carried the day. A department of drama was established in the provincial Education Ministry and endowed with a modest budget. Bill was given a tiny office and, in due course, a secretary-assistant.

He lost no time in bureaucratic formalities but was immediately off and dashing about the province. Neither trains nor automobiles were used on many of these forays as he frequently rode horseback from one place to the next, visiting centres where he felt the roots should be struck. His love for horses was understandable since his most famous appearances in England before coming to Canada involved doing equestrian turns at London theatres under the name "Bronco Bill." His energy and enthusiasm were infectious. Men and women of all ages grasped at the lifeline, glad of any occupation that dispersed gloom and despairing thoughts even if only for an interval. Theatre groups under his direction began to pop up like toadstools.

As time went by it became obvious to the amateur thespians that theatre activity included not only acting and directing but also designing, carpentry, painting, sewing and adapting costumes, lighting, and any number of supernumerary jobs. It brought people together in groups to discuss a variety of subjects other than the Depression. Theatre came to be not only a tool for creating a diversion from anxiety and boredom but also mined a reservoir of unsuspected talent, not only in the field of acting but also in the use of materials for set and stage design, and formerly unsuspected gifts in creative writing.

Archie Fairbairn, Private Secretary at Government House, had long been recognized as a talented watercolourist, but his writing ability was not generally known until two sensitive short plays — one based on west coast Indian folklore — were presented at the provincial festivals in 1933 and 1934. Other resident playwrights who emerged from this movement included Archie MacCorkindale (1934), Reby Edmond, and Connie (Gilmour) Thompson (1936). The work of all showed imagination and their output was quite steady, Reby being notably prolific. At one festival in May of 1935 she had two plays and an adaptation in the six-day event that also offered original scripts by nine other Victorians. Reby's titles were as lyrical as her scripts: *Jewels of the Larucci, The Road From Ancona,* and *Pomegranate House,* to mention three. If anyone could be elected as most likely to succeed in pursuit of a playwright's career it was she, but after she left Victoria for California nothing much more was heard from this talented writer. The intimacy of the British Columbia theatrical scene which had allowed her to grow and develop as a writer appears to have been suppressed in the larger US centres.

By the time I reached my mid-teens, the Major and I had become good friends and soon he was recruiting me for some simple duties during the festival week. Eventually this included helping to organize the Western Canada Theatre Conference breakfast session held annually at the Empress Hotel. This event was always highlighted by a notable figure in the arts world as guest speaker. One year, I recall, it was Hollywood character actor Nigel Bruce and on another occasion legendary Boston Pops maestro Arthur Fiedler.

Much later, near the end of the 1930s, I was asked by Bill to be a zone festival adjudicator. I accepted this challenge with enthusiasm and quite enjoyed it in spite of feeling, now and then, that I should better have been certified a lunatic. Since I adored train travel I found great pleasure in seeing close up for the first time the marvellous diversity and drama of interior British Columbia scenery, to say nothing of meeting dozens of interesting and hospitable people. There was only one bristly confrontation during the three years before I was grounded by becoming a permanent *Times* staffer.

I had seen an inexperienced group present a play whose subject and setting was a funeral. I was curious, on reading the play beforehand, as to how the group was going to approach it. The script trapped a small cast in a static scene on the balcony of the church where the funeral was being held. Dialogue was focused on the person about to be interred and was neither revealing nor touching. It contained no dramatic climax nor even a trace of macabre humour. In fact, there was really nothing there. When performed as part of a three-play evening the production itself was the corpse. No motivation for action of any kind was offered by the script and none was invented by the director in the staging.

It seemed to me that not even a professional cast could pull this one off, so much of the necessary materials of drama being lacking. Gifted actors, especially those who are capable of holding audience attention through their presence and speech alone, can sometimes succeed with little or no stage business, but the more inexperienced the actors, the more they need action to provide them with motivation and to allow them to keep scenes moving. Otherwise they become self-conscious and the lines are likely to resemble a recitation.

These were the points I made in my adjudication, noting that for this inexperienced group the poor script had defeated the novice cast from the outset. At the after-performance meeting with the cast the director buttonholed me with fire in her eye. She challenged me to tell her what I meant by a "good" script and where she could find one. I outlined the components of a script suitable for inexperienced players and suggested a source she should try. At this she gave me the eye again and flung back: "That's where this one came from!"

Considering her obvious lack of either experience or dramatic instinct I resisted the urge to make a speech on the director's first duty being to suit the script to the available cast and technicians. Instead I responded by saying that nothing human is perfect and that even the best source can occasionally turn up a dud.

She was probably having similar thoughts about adjudicators.

There was plenty of evidence that Bullock-Webster's idea worked well overall in combating the general malaise. The festival concept was exactly the right kind of medicine because it provided both mental and physical action and an incentive for hundreds of people whose lives (at the time) were going nowhere. Theatre and music, along with sports, were recognized as mental therapy and were introduced by the authorities into the men's relief camps. I recall being part of a crew that took a Little Theatre play out to the camp at Jordan River, near Sooke. It was appropriately a light comedy that got a great reception and we departed in an atmosphere noticeably lightened, if only temporarily. Such excursions by performing groups of different kinds were frequent and much appreciated.

Bullock-Webster's reign over the province's amateur theatre festival and his assistance in getting the schools drama festival under- way was dynamic and inspiring. All the activity was maintained despite the drama office's staff of two having to cope with the instability of their housing involving twice-a-year moves. Every time the Legislature went into session the community drama office's already inadequate space allotment in the Parliament Buildings was required for occupation by the Speaker of the House. So for an extended period each year the minimal office furnishings of desk, two chairs, and filing cabinet, stock of books, collected stash of loan-out stage curtains, borders, spots and cables had to move out, together with its two-party personnel. Sometimes they found themselves in rented office space in the Stobart Building, in the View Street Central Building, or some other inexpensive and vacant space. "The upheaval was appalling," reminisces the Major's long-term secretary, Anne Adamson. "Everything had to go back when the session prorogued," "with us knowing we'd have to do it all over again in a few months. We always dreaded that event."

To his profound devotion to theatre Bill added his concern for other arts, notably music and the visual arts. He pitched in when the Symphony Society needed him and strongly supported a move initiated by Mark Kearley, a wartime resident of Victoria, to bring together representatives of the Symphony Society and other major arts groups for "the purpose of discussing the possibility of obtaining federal aid for an arts centre after the war." A meeting was held on 25 January 1945, at the Empress Hotel and was well attended by representatives from the Symphony and other arts organizations. The consensus at that meeting was that an arts centre on a small scale should be started as soon as possible, pending what everyone hoped would be a full-scale home for "the arts" springing to life when the war was over. Fifty years later this dream has still not been realized.

Bill continued to be a recognized leader on the provincial scene and a vital force in Victoria's arts world. No one was standing outside his door waiting for the Major to vacate his dais. In fact he was in full swing with no sign of fatigue. Then the bureaucracy discovered he had passed the civil service age for retirement. Immediately, without delay for search or discussion as to who might be a possible successor, he was notified abruptly that he would be retired at the end of the month. He left with understandable bitterness. There was still no clue as to who might take his place. Anne continued to maintain the office's correspondence with the various drama groups, responding to requests from all over the province, shipping and receiving books and production necessities, and giving advice to the best of her ability.

Finally after two or three months had passed with no replacement for Bill within sight, the Department asked him to resume his office temporarily until the right person turned up. Curtly and understandably he refused. After a short stint as aide-de-camp to the Lieutenant-Governor he returned to England permanently with his wife and son and there became involved with movie making. He was a man whose energies refused to be frustrated. He died in England in 1970 at 91.

There were certainly those Victorians who disliked "the Major" for what they considered his "snobbery." Some complained that in public Bill Bullock-Webster often had little time to speak with them although they might have worked quite closely with him. Some saw him as a snob, courting only the big names and the rich.

A time gap of eighteen months was to pass before retired school principal H. S. "Bunny" Hurn, one of the founders of the Victoria

Litttle Theatre, agreed to take over as the province's drama director. Hurn was a man of Welsh ancestry endowed with the Celtic gifts of poetry, cadence and rhythm, and an active imagination. Many of the plays he had selected, directed, and frequently acted in for the Little Theatre are still among the most memorable in that theatre's long history. Those who knew him truly were aware that Hurn was more the dreamer than the forthright activist. The high-gear Bullock-Webster drive was missing in his administration but he cared deeply and his devotion to the cause could never be questioned.

Inevitably there have been adjustments and changes over the years. But the impetus that was achieved and the connective links between theatre groups in all parts of the province through zone festivals, has continued to be an important factor in the leisure and creative aspects of life for hundreds of British Columbians.

One movement which benefitted greatly from the Major's efforts, and in which I was deeply involved, was the Victoria Theatre Guild.

CHAPTER ELEVEN

The Victoria Theatre Guild

IN Victoria after the Second World War there were tentative efforts to establish theatre of a professional or semiprofessional nature. None had had an existence of any length, including a British repertory company directed by Gordon McLeod. On a cross-Canada tour in 1930 this company ran out of funds in Victoria and the players were left to find their way home as best they could. But McLeod, who had lived in Victoria as a child, stayed on and attempted to establish repertory at the old Empire Theatre on Government Street (now the McPherson Playhouse). This also had a life too short to leave anything more than a vague memory.

At the amateur level there was a flourishing and constant activity that epitomized the word, amateur (i.e., for the pleasure of the doing). This is not to suggest that professional performers derive less pleasure from pursuing their art. In fact, more than one professional actor has told me that while he knows his earnings would be greater doing almost anything else he could not easily be wooed away from the theatre.

Small theatre groups have made their contributions everywhere in the civilized world and certainly in Greater Victoria. In addition to the 65-year-old Victoria Theatre Guild the St. Luke's Players has had a long history, although its perspective has changed over the years. It originated as the Doncaster Players, the brainchild of a gifted amateur named Flora Nicholson whose standards were high and whose directorial gifts and dramatic flair were exceptional.

The Theatre Guild is one of the city's true success stories and is among the oldest group of its kind in Canada, having celebrated its 65th birthday in 1994. In addition it is one of the few owning its own theatre complex complete with state-of-the-art stage lighting, well equipped workshop, and superior amenities for active members and audiences. Its active and associate membership rolls have soared to an all-time high of over 1,000, necessitating a production run nearly twice what is was only a few years ago. Threats to its existence over the years, such as the influx of television in the late forties and the development of professional theatre companies, have proved to be more of an incentive toward higher standards than a meek acceptance of inevitable demise.

Victoria Theatre Guild is the title borne by the organization since 1950 but there were two name changes and a revolution prior to that date. This takes us back to how it all began in the fall of 1929 when a group of dedicated amateurs, mainly school teachers who shared a passion for the theatre and an urge to act, got together to discuss the idea of forming an association for the production of quality plays. They soon attracted those of similar interests from other walks of life. Reflecting theatre's classical and medieval origins, the idea crystalized as The Mimes and Masquers Guild. This was a title that did not long survive the jokes that paraphrased it into the "Marms and Masters Guild."

This development paralleled a movement which was developing across Canada for the creation of "little theatre" organizations with the basic goal of reawakening interest in and appreciation for the unique qualities that distinguish the live stage from other dramatic media. The Vancouver Little Theatre was the most westerly of the series of amateur stage revivals until Mimes and Masquers adopted the name Victoria Little Theatre Association in 1933, the year that I joined the organization.

First president of the group under its new name was H. S. "Bunny" Hurn, a school teacher who had been one of the most dedicated members of the originating group. Hurn was an imaginative and able director and totally dedicated to the association. His interest and loyalty never lessened, even when later he became director of the provincial drama department under the Ministry of Education following the retirement of Bill Bullock-Webster.

Among earlier meeting and rehearsal spaces rented by the society was an upstairs barn-like room in a building on lower Yates Street.

Monthly meetings were held there accompanied by off-the-cuff entertainment by various members. In the early days of my membership I recall rainy nights when we sat on hard benches holding open umbrellas to defend us from the leaking rafters. On rehearsal nights actors were often required to duck around under an umbrella while they juggled with props such as beer mugs and cooking pots. A full-length play for public consumption would get one or two rehearsals on the stage of the Shrine Auditorium (later Club Sirocco) or the Empire Theatre (later the McPherson) before being presented to an audience.

A short time later the organization obtained space in one of a pair of now demolished buildings on Burdett Avenue between Linden Avenue and Cook Street. While in a reasonably central location this was still far from adequate for the theatre group either for production or workshop. It became, in fact, simply a meeting place.

A solution, however, was literally just around the corner. On Rockland Avenue, between Linden and Moss Streets, there stood a turn-of-the-century mansion, The Laurels, which had been the residence of the Robert Ward family. It was occupied by various private schools from 1912 until 1928 when it become a lodging house. The property ran back the length of the cul-de-sac now known as Langham Court which connected with the former carriage house, stable, and barn. The carriage house had been used as an assembly hall for the school but now, equipped with light, water, a toilet and an assortment of sad looking wooden chairs, it was rented out to anyone who needed auditorium or rehearsal space. Among its early tenants was the Victoria Operatic Society under the direction of Countess Laura de Turczynowicz which later became the Victoria Civic Opera under Basil Horsfall.

As it happened the president of the Little Theatre, Harry Davis, played flute in the opera orchestra, and quickly saw the possibility of a shared arrangement between the opera and theatre. Thus, the two groups began to share the Langham Court space for rehearsals in 1934 and deemed it the best accommodation they had ever enjoyed. When the opera group obtained their own premises at 1753

106

Rockland in 1937, the Little Theatre was not unhappy to find itself the sole tenant — but not for long for the property was soon put up for sale. Real estate was not moving quickly in 1937, however, and it passed into the city's hands. Once more Davis came to the rescue. From an anonymous theatre-loving couple among his clientele came the offer of an open-ended loan at a minimal interest rate, sufficient for the Little Theatre to purchase the property.

The energy and enthusiasm generated among active members by this windfall brought out all the creativity for which theatre people are well known. A home of their own was for a short while euphoria enough, until the more hard-headed among them began to take inventory of what they were purchasing — a ground-level wooden box without a cellar and a debt stretching well into the future. There was a low platform stage at one end of the hall, virtually no backstage space, and no stage lighting of even the most rudimentary kind. While rehearsals, set construction, and meetings could be held there, public performances had to continue to be held at the Empire Theatre, the Shrine Auditorium on View Street, or the Crystal Garden Theatre. Rental of these facilities was an ongoing financial concern for the executive and only short runs of three or at the most four nights could be afforded.

Thus began the long process of renovating the space so that it could become both a rehearsal and performance facility for the society. This immediately involved installing a new furnace and creating proper dressing rooms below the stage. The glow of achievement, however, sparked further ambition that, over the ensuing years, included improving the back-stage space (including construction of a fly loft), construction of an orchestra pit (later removed to enlarge the stage), installation of a proper lighting switchboard, raking of the audience area to provide better viewing, installation of proper theatre seats obtained from the old Dominion Theatre, and creation of workshop and "Green Room" spaces by connecting the neighboring barn to the theatre. All the work was done by members themselves, and no other project could have done so much to create that atmosphere of mutual appreciation and understanding that permeates the guild even today.

The theatre sustained its activity throughout World War II, producing plays that required mostly female casts. Many plays were repeated without charge for members of the forces, and concerts were organized at Prince Robert House (a military hostel) and on Sunday evenings at Langham Court. In the depression years prior to the war, the Theatre Guild had also shown its civic sense of responsibility by journeying out to the Sooke area to give free performances for men living at the relief camp at Jordan River.

Over these years, a distinct bias developed for the production of typical British farce comedies, such as *Freddy Steps Out*, *Springtime for Henry*, and *Tons of Money*. These were all good for a laugh, but as a steady diet lacked inspiration and challenge for both actors and audiences. Some members began to feel that the choice of plays to be produced was left in the hands of too few executive members (often amounting to only one person). Complaints began to surface from both audience members and the society, about the absence of good Broadway plays and established works by master playwrights. In addition, there was increasing dissatisfaction among directors and some technical staff who felt the theatre was maintaining an artistic standard which was too low. The final indignity was the arbitrary suspension of annual meetings and the resulting lack of information to members of the society, particularly with respect to financial matters. This situation sowed the seed for the one and only revolution among the membership to take place in six decades.

The dissidents took group action by demanding and obtaining an extraordinary general meeting where questions about the absence of annual meetings and resulting detailed reports to the membership were asked. It was then explained that, according to the terms of the "anonymous" loan, so long as the loan was outstanding the original three-man executive was to remain in charge and be solely responsible for the Little Theatre's business affairs. Next there were questions about when the loan would be paid off. The answer given was that, according to acceptable business procedure, when the interest rate was low it was considered wise to pay the interest and let the principal remain on the books until such time as the lender desired to call it in, meanwhile building up theatre funds.

The result of the meeting did nothing to defuse the frustration among some of the membership and a large group of talented and experienced members broke away to form an alternate organization which became known as the Victoria Players Guild. For two seasons this new group made their home at the now vanished Club Sirocco, producing the kind of plays that challenged them and pleased their audiences. These included such classics as *The Barretts of Wimpole Street, The Late George Apley,* and *The Man Who Came to Dinner.* In the summer of 1950 the Players Guild executive was approached by Hurn, who had never forsaken his attachment to the Little Theatre who urged the Players Guild to consider rejoining the Little Theatre.

While some Players Guild members were reluctant, the majority agreed to mend the rupture. Some provisos were made, however: there should be a fresh start with new executive officers and a name change was in order — one that would reflect the original founding name as well as the dissenting group's name. Thus the 1951–52 season ushering in new policies and a strong commitment to the future under the name Victoria Theatre Guild. When the first meeting of the reunited membership was held in the Langham Court Theatre the mood was one of resilience and energy.

The season was an ambitious one, opening with *I Remember Mama* in October followed by six full-length productions included *Hay Fever* and *The Shop at Sly Corner.* The next season was equally full and included *Born Yesterday* and *The Heiress.*

In the 1953-54 season — the 25th — the theatre mortgage was paid off, resulting in funds becoming available for new renovations to the theatre. The stage floor was replaced and levelled and the orchestra pit which had once housed the Little Theatre Orchestra was covered, enlarging the playing area and allowing the new stage curtain to be properly hung. In the lighting switchboard was moved from the wings and established at the rear of the auditorium. The remodelled barn was divided into two areas, the one nearest the stage remaining the workshop and the other, closer to the auditorium, becoming the Percy George Lounge where refreshments are served during performances.

Under its new organizational structure the Guild sailed successfully through problems and crises that would have defeated some crews. Its story has included a number of gifted, resourceful and visionary people who were able to come up with the right answers when the worst problems were threatening. An example was the fire marshal's ultimatum at the end of the 1967–68 season that unless proper fire doors were installed and certain other expensive safety measures taken he would be obliged to terminate the building's use as a theatre.

After exploring the possibility of selling Langham Court — the asking price of $25,000 was a bargain — and particularly of finding another suitable property without success, president Allan Purdy persuaded his board to undertake the necessary alterations using money raised through the sale of debentures to the membership. The response was emphatically affirmative. Most of those who held debentures never bothered to redeem them, and engraved plaques on many of the theatre's seats attest to this generosity. Among those who generously supported this fund-raising project was long-time president Percy George who supplemented the debenture scheme with a large loan. The fire safety alterations were successfully accomplished during the summer months and the theatre — with official blessings — was able to open for the fall season with Arthur Kopit's *Oh, Dad, Poor Dad, Mamma's Hung You in the Closet and I'm Feeling So Sad,* only a few weeks late.

A collaboration between the Theatre Guild and the University of Victoria theatre department was begun in the early seventies before the present Phoenix Theatre was built. There was no space for storage of sets and props within the perimeter of the UVIC grounds so an arrangement was made with the Theatre Guild for storage space at Langham Court. This led to a mutually benefitial relationship between the two establishments which eventually involved theatre students carrying out some of their assignments at the Langham Court theatre.

Even more enriching to all concerned were the shared productions by UVIC and the Guild. These included a fine production of Bertolt Brecht and Kurt Weil's *The Threepenny Opera* with a cast headed by John Krich, Judy Treloar, and Helen Smith which was also played in St. John's, Newfoundland at the invitation of Theatre Canada. Other joint productions with UVIC were Shakespeare's *Much Ado About Nothing* and *The Merchant of Venice*. Mary-Jane Scott, who worked for both organizations, was an important link in these developments.

In the mid-70s UVIC theatre director John Krich and lighting expert Giles Hogya supervised the purchase and installation of a new lighting system. In 1978 Helen Smith, who had served the Guild well in many capacities, made a large donation to pay for the rebuilding and extension of the lobby to its present form. Throughout the eighties the pace of improvements has not slowed while the Guild has continued with unbroken successions of six productions each season as well as numerous and often successful festival entries.

I joined the Little Theatre in 1933 and my first responsibility was "props," a job most people liked to avoid. For me the challenge, particularly in period plays, overcame my natural reluctance to ask for favours. Anyone who is interested in taking up theatre should realize that there are many important and interesting functions apart from acting. Backstage or offstage aspects can be fascinating and satisfying, and are so essential to the effectiveness of any production. So I was absorbed and happy with my role in those early days and learned a good deal through observing and analysing what other people did on stage and off.

The first full-length production for which I was responsible for hand props was John Galsworthy's class-clash play, *The Skin Game*. Fred Spencer, a well-known Victoria businessman and generally good-natured, joined the Little Theatre because he liked to act. He hailed from Yorkshire, and the role of the factory owner in this play was considered ideal for him.

The dress rehearsal took place on stage at the Empire and I, of course, was there early arranging the furniture that had been brought in and setting up a table in the wings for hand props that had to be carried on during the course of the play. When that was done I looked forward to going out front and watching the performance, but before the curtain was to open on Act I the director handed me another job. The prompter was ill and the director asked if would I take the book. So there I was behind the stage-right drop anxiously moving my finger along the lines as they were spoken. Suddenly there was silence in the midst of a confrontation between Fred and his antagonists. I looked up, saw him standing there, glaring but silent, and gave him the cue in a loud whisper. At this he swung round facing the wings and shouted "Shut up!"

I was shaken. Had I been wrong? Was he supposed to take a pause at that spot? No, the director later told me, it's Fred. "He likes to take a pause when he feels it'll be effective. I've tried to talk him out of it but he goes deaf when it suits him."

This was nice for the other actors, I thought, but there was no questioning his egotism. On another much later occasion when I was directing Noel Coward's *Still Life* in a programme of Coward's short plays the excellent character actress Gwen Downes was paired with Fred in cameo roles. The first night went off well but on the second Gwen uncharacteristically fluffed some lines following Fred's entry. Back stage I couldn't tell why this unprecedented stumble had occurred. But after the final curtain the mystery was solved when she confronted Fred with great indignation. "Don't you ever do that again"! She pointed to his tie which was a particularly aggressive scarlet with blue spots. It seemed he had decided to change ties for the second performance and had done so without telling her or showing it to her beforehand. When her eyes fell on it as they started their scene together it had distracted her to the point of momentarily losing her lines. Later I understood that no experienced or professional actor makes a change in stage business or regalia without drawing the attention of those sharing the scene.

From my vantage point backstage I had the perfect opportunity to watch many directors at work. It appeared to me that some directors approached the task of interpreting a playscript by simply copying, detail for detail, stage directions printed in the script. It occurred to me that two intelligent and imaginative directors should be able to find very different values in the same script and, in interpreting it, present individual concepts. A few years later, when I was directing Noel Coward's one act *Family Album* as a Little Theatre festival entry, a member of the cast who had previously worked with a professional English repertory company challenged me concerning positions and movement on stage. He complained that the set differed markedly from the original as illustrated in the published script. This was indeed so. In order to establish a Victorian-era atmosphere for the opening tableau-like scene, we (my husband, Maurice, was in charge of set design and construction) had moved an insignificant door leading to assumed parts of the house from its centre position in the script's layout to stage right. To replace it at centre Maurice designed a triple-arched period window heavily draped in the Victorian fringed and tasselled mode.

The first line in the play was spoken by a young member of the family peering between the drawn folds of curtain commenting on the rain, an atmospheric remark considering that the family had gathered following the funeral of "dear Papa." Midway down stage and slightly stage right we placed a curving-backed Victorian sofa upon which, as the curtain rose, were seated two hoop-skirted ladies slowly turning the pages of a family album.

The actor playing the manservant who was to make his first entrance through the door demanded of me how I, an amateur, could justify changing the original "professional" design. Probably what troubled him most was that we had de-emphasized his entrance by moving him away from centre, a quite natural reaction on his part. But there is no law that says we, having paid for the production rights, cannot make changes even to the cutting of whole scenes or playing on a bare stage. At the festival, incidentally, our *Family Album* won first place. The adjudicator gave high praise to the opening tableau and other aspects of the production. In fact, he confessed he could not find fault with any aspect of setting, performance, and direction.

To satisfy my own instincts and to discover more precisely the techniques of script construction and directing, in 1937 I enrolled in a summer theatre course, dealing largely with play writing, at the

Banff School of Fine Arts with Lister Sinclair. What I learned during those six weeks was a revelation and laid a groundwork and was followed by further study in 1945 at a UBC Theatre Department summer school with instructors Dorothy Somerset, Sydney Risk, and others.

Sometimes we seem to be blessed with exceptional luck in attracting a rare and special talent to create a miracle for us. I was once asked to choose and direct a play for the Theatre Guild's entry into the Dominion Drama Festival. My choice fell on *The Heiress*, a play adapted from the Henry James novel, *Washington Square*. The setting represented an opulent residence of the early Victorian era — heavy draperies, an elegant staircase, a handsome marble mantel displaying exquisite ormolu, and porcelain ornaments.

My husband, Maurice, in charge of set construction, had working with him several regular Guild backstage workers and a relative newcomer of somewhat difficult temperament. His name was John Keane and he was as difficult as he could be. He was a descendant of a famous Irish artist whose talents, to a considerable degree, he had inherited. Among other items, he painted a handsome portrait and installed it in a Baroque frame to hang in the staircase alcove. We were all impressed, but more was to come. It so happened that he had met a city engineer directing a crew in the vicinity. Through him he made friends with Mrs. Mary O'Reilly, the owner of the heritage Point Ellice House. Hearing that we were badly in need of some period furnishings she unhesitatingly invited John and me to visit her and indicate whatever we would like to borrow! The fact that her precious furnishings would require to be transported to Vancouver where the regional Dominion Drama Festival Finals were taking place appeared neither to trouble her nor bother John. I was apprehensive, to say the least, but had not the wisdom to point out that her insurance company (if any) might well have something to say. I did find myself carefully avoiding comment on pieces I admired but recognized as priceless for fear that she might insist on us taking them.

When she went out to make tea John nudged me as he pointed to a mantel populated with bric-a-brac that was obviously Chelsea

114

or something equally historic and virtually priceless. I dug my heels in and insisted that no reference should be made to these collector's items. John complied, which was highly unusual for him, and we left with the understanding that three elegant Victorian side chairs and a lovely table were to be picked up the following day. We were doing a trial run of *The Heiress* for a Theatre Guild audience at Langham Court before taking the production to Vancouver for festival competition. On the morning of the night of our first performance Maurice and John and other crew members were hard at work putting finishing touches to the set and fine-tuning the lighting. I arrived in the theatre about 10 a.m., walking through the foyer into the crossover where I stopped to admire what was quite honestly a handsome, in fact opulent *mise en scène*. My eyes wandered about the stage and then my heart missed a beat — the Baroque fireplace was elegant, especially its ornate mantel furnished with — O, please God, no! — exquisite bric-a-brac that could only have come from Point Ellice House.

I charged up to the stage, for once matching John Keane's own intemperate rages. "John!" I shouted. "Where's John?" Then I got a close view of that mantel and realized that what I was looking at was brilliant fakery. The formations, the luscious colour, the sheen, was nothing but scraps garnered from the workshop floor and castaway bins — porcelain insulators, oddments of wood and metal, and cardboard — all put together into semblances of elegant shapes and painted and varnished to a lustre.

Mine was not the only eye deceived. We were declared the winners of the BC regional competition but the laurels bestowed by international adjudicator Pierre Lefevre went particularly to the staging, special mention being made of the aura created by a soft light on the curtain before it rose. "The curtain should never be dark in the interval before it rises," said LeFevre. "This is the first time I have seen it so professionally done in this festival." That praise belonged to Maurice as stage manager just as the praise for the setting was earned by John Keane. The play also won best actress award for Helen Smith, a newcomer to Victoria from Ottawa. She was destined to become a major figure in the city's theatrical activity and one of the most widely known amateur thespians in Canadian theatre. *The Heiress*, incidentally, was awarded the brand-new Eric Hamber trophy as the best show in the festival — the first and last time the trophy was awarded for that purpose.

At the usual after-show party many people remarked that it was quite apparent where the entry came from: "It could only be Victoria with all those lovely antiques and china," we were told.

There is a postscript to this incident. Winning the regional for British Columbia automatically admitted us to the finals to be held that year (1952) in Saint John, New Brunswick. That possibility, of course, should have been discussed and taken in hand even before casting and rehearsals were begun since the expenses had to be met by the Theatre Guild. As it was the Guild executive decided that no effort could be undertaken to raise the necessary travel funds. It was not surprising that Vancouver's DDF regional executive was indignant since that decision eliminated the province altogether from the finals.

While amateur theatre was developing among those who engaged in the activity "for the love of it," professional theatre made important contributions to the cultural life of the city.

CHAPTER TWELVE

Early Professional Theatre

HILE a stock company composed largely of local professionals had been successfully operated by Reginald Hincks in the 1920s, the first full-scale professional repertory theatre adventure in the city was the brainchild of the young actor-writer-director, Ian Thorne.

Thorne had left his native England in the late 1940s to take a teaching post at the Qualicum School for Boys. His true literary interest was not so much vested in English writings confined between book covers as it was in English and American works for the theatre. With his real intent in view he chose and prepared, with his students, the first act of Thornton Wilder's inspired cartoon on the twentieth- century human condition, *Skin of Our Teeth*, as his entry in the 1950 Victoria Drama Festival. The performance was done with zest and comprehension and won awards. I met him for the first time at the reception following the festival.

After I had congratulated him on the success of his entry he drew me aside. He admitted that he had taken the teaching post purely for the sake of being admitted to Canada and went on to say that he was not really interested in teaching as a career. His purpose from the outset, he boldly stated, was to establish himself in a Canadian city as the director of a theatre company. In this there was no conceit for he was trained and experienced in theatre although still in his twenties.

His object in entering the festival was to get him to Victoria where he hoped to meet prominent and theatrically interested people to help him get started on his repertory project. His eye was trained on the then closed and deteriorating York Theatre (now the MacPherson Playhouse) and his mind was set on finding a backer to rent it and a "patsy" to put together a cast and start rehearsals. I found out later that I had been pre-selected by him as the patsy, partly because of my active connection with the Little Theatre and also because I was a provincial adjudicator. He had it all carefully worked out — I would get the project rolling and he would take over from me when school holidays started. I didn't need anyone's advice to turn the proposal down. I could imagine my editor's reaction and my own dubious position if I took on such a project. I told him I would do what I could for him but hands-on participation was out.

By the time the summer of 1952 had arrived Thorne had acquired financial assistance from a bedazzled young man who had recently come into an inheritance, and he began negotiations for rental of the theatre. There followed some cleaning up and marginal work of a cosmetic nature while Thorne proceeded with the formation of a repertory company. This included some experienced Victoria actors, a few of whom had been on the professional stage, and a few as guest stars from the quite excellent semi-professional Portland (Oregon) Civic Theatre.

Opening night arrived. The interior of the old York had been freshly painted and handsome crystal chandeliers had been acquired to dress up the foyer. All female first-nighters were presented with white roses, the emblem of the Royal house of York. For the occasion these had been specially flown in from Hawaii.

The vehicle was a frothy comedy by the fruitful, if trite, British playwright Philip King titled *On Monday Next*, but appropriately renamed "Curtain Up" by Thorne. Directing and also playing the role of the director was Thorne who, judging from the subsequent reviews, did a fine job of both. The audience included Premier W. A. C. and Mrs. Bennett and the opening commentary was given by the vice-president of the company, one-time city alderman Geoff Edgelow.

The York Company as well as guest artists from Vancouver, Seattle, and Portland, included names still familiar to many Victoria theatre buffs. Among these were Elizabeth Knight, better known

118

in more recent Victoria theatre history as Betty Mayne, and Victoria's late multi-talented thespians Vivienne Chadwick and Gwen Downes. All would have fit into any professional company's cast.

Thorne's plan was to establish a true "stock" company, changing plays on a weekly basis and presenting them as fall, winter, and spring series. He maintained a policy of choosing only Broadway and West End successes and began attracting a faithful audience, although considerably smaller than had been anticipated considering the company had no professional rivals in the city. Regulars included a promising segment of out-of-towners. Then on an early fall evening in 1953 it all collapsed.

Why were people milling about outside the locked main doors of the theatre? Some had made the journey down from Duncan. Hand printed signs pasted up on the doors told part of the story: the company had gone on strike, having not been paid for weeks. Typical theatre professionals of the time would endure much in the way of long hours, late nights, and moderate delays in pay which most other workers would not accept. One actor commented in an interview with me: "I would rather act and have a life in the theatre than earn more money doing something that was just a daily chore." The Canadian Actors' Equity Association (CAEA) has altered the situation considerably since then.

It turned out that behind the collapse was a tragi-comedy of colossal financial ineptitude with not only the company rebelling, but with many of the York's suppliers uttering the usual threats. The funds that had allowed Thorne and his friends to launch their enterprise had been flushed away with extravagance and that was the end of the story. A carton stuffed with unopened and unpaid bills was found underneath the box office counter. No one sued because there was no one to be sued. So ended the York episode, but waiting in the wings were its successors. The first of these took the historic coupling with York, choosing Lancaster for their title. The company included a number of the original members of the York Players but under-funding and public disillusionment brought an early conclusion to this effort.

Thorne went on to make a name for himself as a writer and director, first in Vancouver, later at the Shaw Festival and in Toronto, and finally in England, where perhaps his most significant contribution was his involvement as a writer for the *Six Wives of Henry the Eighth* television series. He returned to Toronto in the 1970s and died there in 1978.

At that time there were some noteworthy theatrical talents at work in Vancouver using the name Totem Theatre. Its partners were Thor Arngrim and Stuart Baker, with pixie-faced Norma MacMillan as a leading lady. Sometime playwright Peter Mannering (later to found Bastion Theatre in Victoria) was a director-actor with the company. Their repertoire consisted of light popular plays of the era and their audiences were growing when their green light turned suddenly to red. The old wooden building in which they staged their in-the-round productions had been condemned for public use by the Vancouver authorities.

Totem had to close down after only two years while Arngrim and Baker frantically sought another possible venue. It was just at this time that news of the York Theatre's demise reached Vancouver. What's in a city? Theatre people will locate and perform wherever they can find a space with four walls, a roof that doesn't leak, and an audience.

Arngrim, Baker, and company migrated to Victoria and happily took over the dilapidated rat-haunted old theatre to which McPherson in his lifetime paid little heed but which was later to be graced with his name. Down came the York sign and up went the Totem marquee, but the Totem venture was even shorter lived than the York. Mannering, who shared directing assignments with Sam Payne, was a widely admired and experienced professional Vancouver actor-director. He was quoted in a feature article in the *Globe and Mail*, describing the Totem Theatre as being "in a slum area" where many people were afraid to venture at night. In fact there were no bad slum areas in Victoria in the early fifties and street crime, unlike in the decades of the eighties and nineties, was almost unknown.

Nevertheless, the situation of the structure — its dilapidation in the midst of a comparatively drab neighbourhood — did keep many potential theatre-goers home. Nearby was the old public market lodged in a former fire hall and a block or two away was a shabby but historic Chinatown. On the east-facing perimeter was a rather drab version of our present city hall.

The theatre's capacity at that time, including the perilously raked balcony, was close to 900 seats (in 1963 alterations reduced the seating capacity to 837). A "good house," from the box office perspective, averaged around 700 with a little more than half being on the main floor. During its tenure Totem often attracted no more than 100 persons a night despite a programme of well-done, light, effervescent plays shaped to what appeared to be the average audience taste. The company was made up largely of main-stream Vancouver actors who had talent, experience, and charm. But none of this it seemed, could overcome the theatre's disadvantages. Thus 1954 saw the end of Totem's one and only season. Nevertheless, the Totem Theatre experience was to sow the seed for a future and much stronger and longer-lasting growth which would become the Bastion Theatre of British Columbia.

The company broke up and scattered: Arngrim went to Toronto and from there to New York where he and Norma MacMillan were married and both continued in the entertainment industry, especially in television. The remainder of the company returned to Vancouver, including Mannering who helped found the Holiday Playhouse for children before going to England where he worked in London's Arts Theatre for a year. He also had seasons at Ontario's Stratford Festival and from there, at John Hirsch's invitation, he went to Winnipeg's Manitoba Theatre Centre.

It was in Winnipeg in 1962 that Mannering heard the news: Thomas Shanks McPherson had died leaving his decaying old Pantages-Coliseum-Empire-York-Totem theatre to the City of Victoria, together with a bequest of some four million dollars for its renovation and beautification. The theatre, he directed, was to be used primarily for the occupation and pleasure of the citizens of Greater Victoria.

By the time Mannering was made aware of the bequest work had already begun on the initial phase of renewal. A citizen's committee, comprising Allan Purdy, Jack Barraclough, Maurice, and myself had been chosen by City Council to work with and advise the architect, Alan Hodgson.

Mannering was born on the west coast and had grown up in Vancouver. He yearned for his natural environment and a theatre where he could develop and direct his own company. He recognized the fact that someone on the spot and known in the city would have the best chance of installing a resident company in the born-again theatre. So he determined to leave Winnipeg for Victoria without delay. Despite Hirsch's warning about Victoria's poor record as a theatre town and his effort to persuade Mannering to remain in Winnipeg, Peter packed his bags and was on his way.

His plans were made known to a group of theatre-minded citizens when Anne Adamson, still with the Department of Education's Drama Division, hosted an evening reception for him. There Mannering told his audience how he intended to proceed by establishing a theatre school for all ages and a bare-bones informal presentation of plays. From some of those present came information about a former church, then disused, which might be, and indeed was, available for his purpose. This was a similar but somewhat smaller building than the Fernwood church that is now the Belfry Theatre. He was soon installed in his new "digs" and people were signing up, including pre-schoolers, secondary school students and adults. People who attended Peter's "capsule" versions of classic plays were happy with what they saw and an atmosphere of vitality and general enthusiasm pervaded the enterprise which was the chrysalis stage of the Bastion Theatre.

Whether known as the Pantages, Coliseum, Empire, York, or McPherson Playhouse, that building at the corner of Government and Pandora played a larger part in theatre developments in Victoria than most historians give it credit for.

❧

Performance of *The Duchess of Malfi* for Victoria Fair, 1970, showing (front) John Krich and Wandalie Henshaw (John Krich)

b–i

Performance of *Justice Not Revenge* for Victoria Fair, 1971, showing (front) Duncan Regehr, Richard Galuppi, Eric Schneider, Harriet Allen, Harvey M. Miller, Maria Wozniak, and John Krich (John Krich)

Kaleidoscope's Story Theatre on the road. Pictured are Sheryl Fjellgaard, Mark Hellman, David McLeod, and Lorna Olafson. (Kaleidoscope Theatre, E. M. Johnson)

Elizabeth Gorrie and Friend, 1983 (Bill Halkett, Victoria *Times-Colonist*)

Cast of *Yeomen of the Guard* directed by Audrey Johnson for the Victoria Gilbert and Sullivan Society, May 1958. (E. M. Johnson)

Production of *Amahl and the Night Visitors*, Christ Church Cathedral, December 1959, with (l. to r.) Timothy Vernon, Peggy Walton Packard, Ian Willox, Norman Tyrrell, Harry Johns, and Stanley Hoban. (Peggy Walton Packard)

Cast of *Dido and Aeneas* at Oak Bay Junior High School, January 1961, directed by Audrey Johnson (3rd from right) and conducted by Boyce Gaddes (2nd from right). Also shown are Peggy Walton Packard (seated), Jock Dunbar, Norman Tyrell, Adele (Gould) Lewis, and others. (Jorgen V. Svendsen)

Cast of *Gianni Schicchi*, produced by the Victoria Musical Art Society, May 1962, directed by Audrey Johnson (right) and conducted by James Gayfer (left). Also pictured are Norman Tyrrell, Erika Kurth, Eleanor Duff, Adele (Goult) Lewi,, Hans Steffan, Peggy Walton Packard, and others. (Robin Clarke, E. M. Johnson)

Cast of *Murder in the Cathedral* at Christ Church Cathedral, November 1966. Actors pictured include Allan Purdy, Michael Meiklejohn, John Britt, John Drean, Richard Litt, and Gerald Webb. (Robin Clarke, E. M. Johnson)

Cast of *Hadrian VII* directed by Allan Purdy and Audrey Johnson at Christ Church Cathedral, February, 1973, with John Heath (centre) as Fr. Rolfe. (Hans F. Dietrich, E. M. Johnson)

Barabara Collier and Richard
Margison in *The Elixir of Love*,
September 1983. (Alex Barta, Victoria *Times-Colonist*)

Soprano and sculptress Peggy
Walton Packard, April 1957. (Jim
Ryan, Victoria *Times-Colonist*)

Allan Purdy, April 1981. (Bill
Halkett, Victoria *Times-Colonist*)

Colin Graham, Founding Curator, Art Gallery of Greater Victoria, 1951–1973. (Ken McAllister,
Art Gallery of Greater Victoria)

b–ix

W. E. "Bill" West pictured in front of his installation at the Dan George Theatre, University of Victoria, January 1985. (Alex Barta, Victoria *Times-Colonist*)

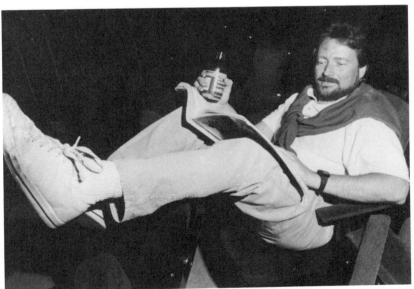

Timothy Vernon, Artistic Dirctor of Pacific Opera Victoria, 1980–95. (John McKay, Victoria *Times-Colonist*)

Formal Opening by Governor-General Viscount Alexander of the Little Centre at Thomas Plimley's auto showroom, 965 Yates Street, 19 July 1946. (Art Gallery of Greater Victoria)

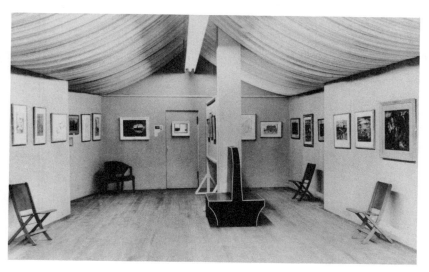

Art Centre of Greater Victoria at 825 Broughton Street, c1950. (W. Atkins, British Columbia Press Agency)

The Spencer Mansion on Moss Street, c1951, when it was about to become the Art Gallery of Greater Victoria (Ken McAllister, Art Gallery of Greater Victoria)

Victoria *Times-Colonist* cartoonist Adrian Raeside spoofs Audrey's career. (Adrian Raeside, Victoria *Times-Colonist*)

The McPherson Playhouse

T almost the same time as the new Royal Victoria Theatre was about to open (1913) a well-known entrepreneur of the American vaudeville stage, Alexander Pantages, purchased a lot in the 1600-block of Government Street and built there one of a string of theatres which bore his name. The Pantages, as we have already seen, was destined to have a more patchwork career than the Royal, the latter's ups and downs notwithstanding.

Because its primary function was as a vaudeville house the Pantages was built without certain otherwise necessary facilities such as an orchestra pit of sufficient dimensions for productions other than simple comedy acts or revues. Nor was sufficient consideration given to backstage requirements for larger productions. Similar criticisms can, even now, be applied to the Royal, although recent alterations have much improved the front-of-house areas. Thus, despite extensive renovations, both theatres have remained, as the twentieth century moves to its close, lacking in certain vital back and front stage requirements.

The Pantages, following the gradual demise of vaudeville, was to become a main stage for Victoria Little Theatre in the 1930s, home to two professional repertory companies in the fifties, and, most astounding of all, a meeting house for a fractured Methodist congregation led by the charismatic preacher Clem Davies in the mid-twenties. This sandy-haired, short-in-stature Welshman who possessed a magnetic personality and gift of oratory, filled the house from pit-line to the eagle-perch backrow of the gallery every Sunday for months. Davies was proof that the inspirational preacher and the inspired actor are brothers under the skin. The family's theatrical bent was later to be further demonstrated through Davis's only daughter, Dorothy, who became a well-known theatre professional in Vancouver.

When Pantages's empire collapsed as Hollywood made inroads into popular entertainment the Government Street theatre became an occasional roadshow or local production spot and slid gradually into mouldy, rat-haunted obsolescence. During this period it was variously re-christened by different owners and renters as the Coliseum (1925), the Empire (1932), the York (1941), and the Totem (1953). Coming perilously near to encountering the wrecking ball in the seventies, it was to survive with distinction in the centuries' closing years, as the McPherson Playhouse in honour of the man who bequeathed it to the city.

When the date for the formal opening of the fully-renovated theatre had been established, the city fathers made the problematical decision to hold a contest and invite proposals from those interested in creating the grand opening. They had also made a wise move to hire a manager for the theatre well ahead of time, thus providing that person with a chance of getting to know the city and its inhabitants.

The contest brought suggestions and offers from many city groups and individuals. But it appeared inevitable that Mannering, with his professional theatre background, would be selected to mastermind the project. His proposal was for a mixed programme of comedy, drama, dance, and music, each item to be in the hands of some recognized group or individual with himself as overall producer.

With his prime interest and maximum efforts directed at the development of a theatre school and the creation of a resident professional theatre company with the McPherson as its base, he took on a heavy load. He had little time to supervise the progress of the grand opening and keep the clock ticking on the various groups and individuals who were to constitute that programme. With the McPherson's widely-touted curtain-raising not much more than a couple of weeks away he finally was able to find the time to execute a round of inspection. He came to the horrifying realization that

124

several phases of the programme seemed to have fallen apart. Further, it appeared that no one was poised and ready to fill the gaps at that juncture.

He took this dilemma to the new manager who, unfortunately, devised the worst possible scenario. Panicking, he called Famous Artists in Vancouver to see if they could conjure up a professional act that might be available on that crucial opening night.

It appeared that the only personality who was likely to be available on such short notice was doing nightclub appearances in Los Angeles. She was Elsa Lanchester, widow of Charles Laughton, and known as a capable if not outstanding character actress. She agreed to come and since invited guests from as far away as Toronto, Winnipeg, Portland, and Seattle, as well as provincial government officials and Government House were to be present, immense sighs of relief wafted through City Hall. Some of us, however, had seen Lanchester's one-woman performance at the Royal in the previous season. Far from being impressed we were, to put it mildly, apprehensive. A cocktail reception was arranged for Lanchester at City Hall after she had been given a tour of the theatre. I was introduced to her as the *Times* theatre reviewer. She looked at me with anxious little-girl eyes and said: "I only hope I'm good enough for your lovely theatre." Prophetic words, for she wasn't, not by any effort of imagination no matter how charitable one wished to be.

The art of the solo performer in the theatre requires extraordinary gifts of imagination, intensity, and projection. These gifts go well beyond the capabilities of the average support player on stage or screen. This is especially the case when one has to hold the attention and interest of a full house for a minimum of 80 to 90 minutes. Such a challenge can only be fielded by an artist with a compelling personality and superb dramatic range, or a comedian who needs no help to maintain a steady flow of jokes, mime, and sight-gags to keep an audience in its seats and in an uproar for a couple of hours.

It is not required that one be overly sensitive or highly knowledgeable to be aware of the low temperature, the flatness, in a performance that is going nowhere. Embarrassment as the grand opening collapsed like a castle of cards was plainly etched on every civic face as they left the handsomely restored theatre's first night. Someone had to pay and the manager was the victim, being summarily dismissed from a job in which he had barely wet his toes.

As it turned out "opening night" could well have highlighted Victoria's own show after all. The Monday following the weekend opening the Mac's handsome new curtain finally rose on *Lights Up*. This was a substantial programme that presented an array of the city's best performers and ensembles all the way from George Fairfield's orchestra to a large chorus under the direction of James Gayfer, then director of the HMCS *Naden* School of Music.

The body of the programme included nibbles at Shakespeare — excerpts from the musical *Kiss Me Kate* as well as from its source, *Taming of the Shrew*, with University of Victoria's Carl Hare as Grumio and gifted Theatre Guild actress Margaret Hall as Kate. Popular stand-up comedian Jerry Gosley provided his hilarious Captain Vancouver "Looking at Victoria" act. There was dance, classic and modern — *Scotland on Stage* with authentic Scottish dancing was directed by Adeline Duncan, a *Brigadoon* episode was choreographed by Wynne Shaw, and dancers coached by talented teacher-choreographer Vivian Briggs presenting *French Canada on Stage*. Other show-business classics and play excerpts were also presented.

Also on the *Lights Up* program, as a piano accompanist, was teenaged Timothy Vernon. Timothy had hovered between music and theatre as a career, until he became a member of a summer school class for conductors given by Otto-Werner Mueller at the new School of Music. Mueller considered Vernon rather young for the class (he would have been about 16 at the time) but nevertheless accepted him on the basis of his innate musicality. That decision on Mueller's part would later settle the teenager's long-term future. His next long stride was to the Vienna Academy of Music where he studied for four years with the aid of Canada Council grants, graduating *cum laude*. From that achievement he went to Italy where he studied operatic conducting under maestro, Franco Ferara. Today Vernon teaches and conducts at McGill University but is also known across Canada and applauded in his home town as the music director-conductor of Pacific Opera Victoria.

Most of those attending the Bastion Theatre Studio's all-Victoria production were left wondering why on earth it had not been given the gala opening spotlight. Its appropriateness and numerous noteworthy acts would easily have compensated for the occasional weaker moments.

After *Lights Up*, the Victoria Symphony Society and the new Victoria School of Music (later to become the Conservatory of Music) presented a concert which featured the Victoria Choral Society and professionally hopeful chamber group the Amity Singers with the Victoria Symphony Orchestra in a performance of Mozart's *Requiem Mass in D minor*. This was dedicated to the memory of benefactor Thomas S. McPherson and conducted by Otto-Werner Mueller.

The opening weeks at the McPherson continued through the spring with a variety of musical and dramatic events. These included the Vancouver Playhouse Company's production of Jean Anouilh's *Ring Round the Moon*, Spanish dancer Susana y Jose, the Seattle Repertory Company performing *Twelfth Night* and O'Neill's *Ah, Wilderness*. This was followed by Bastion Theatre Studio's first full production at the McPherson, the long-lived comedy, *Life With Father*, starring the well-known Vancouver actor, Sam Payne. The cast also included Margaret Martin, later to become famous on television and stage in the role of Emily Carr.

An interim manager was appointed for the McPherson but left after a fairly short stay and within a few months two exciting events took the new theatre's destiny in hand. The engagement of Vancouver's John Dyck as manager made a significant difference to the community status, direction, and character of the theatre. Here was someone who brought imagination and multi-dimensional views to the operation and who made the facility come alive. John perceived his role not simply as a bookkeeper, but as an initiator of ideas and innovative usage of the facility. During his tenure he encouraged participation from a wide cross-section of the community.

How far he might have been able to pursue his vision under ordinary civic bureaucracy is hard to predict, but two Victoria businessmen were in the wings and at precisely the right moment stepped forward. Lunching together one day, Alderman Ron McKenzie (who chaired the Cultural Committee on city council) was telling Allan Purdy about grumbling at council meetings concerning the city being "saddled" with the operation of a theatre. He felt that sooner or later they were going to seek a way to dump this responsibility.

There were few angles to theatre management that Allan did not know since he had been born to parents in the professional theatre and had once managed a playhouse at Croydon, England. Before emigrating to Canada he had also managed his own repertory company after being demobilized from the RAF bomber command. At that chance luncheon meeting he laid out a plan on a paper napkin by which the onus of administration would be taken off city council and put in the hands of a council-appointed board of citizens that would include two council representatives. McKenzie was impressed and asked Purdy to put his proposal in a form that could be officially presented to Council. This was speedily done and with the majority of council in favour, the controlling body was subsequently registered under the title McPherson Playhouse Foundation. Purdy was the inevitable choice to head it, with other members of the board including an accountant, a lawyer, John Goult, alderman McKenzie, manager John Dyck, and myself.

It would be difficult to replicate a group demonstrating such excellent relationships, dedication, and understanding as this one. Each board member understood the importance of the theatre's survival and genuinely cared about it. Each also fully understood City Council's concerns while desiring to satisfy McPherson's wish that the theatre be a place for the joy and profit of all citizens of Victoria. All not only respected but relished the ideas and involvement of the manager.

The success of the McPherson was due in great measure to Dyck's presence, his insight and creativity, and his excellent rapport. This applied not only with the Foundation but also with the dedicated technical head, Lawrence Eastick, and all front- and back-stage personnel. The McPherson rapidly became, and sustained throughout Dyck's presence, a vibrancy and warmth.

Among the more memorable events at the theatre were those presented by various schools. When Dyck heard of some Greater Victoria school having prepared and performed an especially well-done stage production he would go to see it himself. If the presentation were of sufficient quality he would invite teachers and students to give a special performance at the McPherson. Thereby the students gained the experience of performing in a real theatre with a professional stage crew, lighting, and other effects. Frequently some profit would result from the venture, and the school went home with its share to be put towards needed stage equipment.

The McPherson was alive and thriving, a friendly, open place where many kinds of activities were carried out, including art shows in the foyer and free noon-hour concerts made possible by the local chapter of the American Federation of Musicians. There was also children's entertainment and impressive craft shows. The end to much of this came, unfortunately, when the City of Vancouver called on John Dyck to become manager of that city's three theatres — the Queen Elizabeth, the Playhouse, and the New Orpheum. All were sunk in a depression and showing red on the city's books. The call was too great a challenge for John to resist.

Vancouver's gain was our distinct loss. The McPherson reverted to being simply a commercial property lacking the vision and the exploratory role it had played so successfully. In accordance with its bylaws the membership of the Foundation board changed at regular intervals, but without a leader comparable to Dyck the McPherson ceased to be a vibrant centre for the exploration and development of ideas and settled into the routine role of a rental house. As home to the Bastion Theatre, however, it continued to play an important role in the Victoria arts community.

CHAPTER FOURTEEN

The Bastion Theatre

*B*ASTION Theatre grew from its modest beginning with unexpected rapidity and, initially, minimal funding. Like most theatres it experienced anxious times but there were also those that were buoyant, and even triumphant. It drew the attention of the Ottawa and Toronto press and was being referred to as "Bastion Theatre of Canada." It collapsed on the eve of celebrating its silver anniversary, sending shock waves through theatre communities far and wide.

The first full-length production by Bastion at the McPherson was the comedy classic, *Life With Father* by Howard Lindsay and Russel Crouse. It was directed by Peter Mannering and was a pleasing performance that sent the audience out of the theatre in a happy mood, but the big joke was on the reviewers of both Victoria dailies. We knew each other well, but never compared notes, mainly because the *Colonist* reporter often disappeared before the final curtain since he had to rush back to his office to make the midnight deadline. On this occasion we both commented, in print, on the obvious "wig" worn by the eldest son (according to the script, like the Father, he is a redhead) as being overly bright, thick, and unbelievable. Otherwise, we agreed, actor Barry Flatman was excellent in the role. That morning the real mother of the youngster phoned me, choking with laughter. The "wig" was quite honestly Barry's own natural growth, untinted and unfortified!

Incidentally, Flatman developed his talent with Bastion Theatre School and went on to being an Canadian Actors' Equity member with plenty of work in and about Toronto. A number of young actors from Bastion's school have entered professional ranks, among them Andrew Sabiston.[1] He is the son of Carole Sabiston, one of Victoria's most original and internationally noted artists.

During its first full season of production Bastion achieved an attendance figure of 2,000 for seven shows. The goal for the second season, 1966-67, was set at 4,000. At the close of the first season a woman whose name was to become virtually synonymous with Bastion Theatre, became its first full-time office manager — Helen Simpson-Baikie. Her arrival coincided with the first grant from Victoria City Council which consisted of thirteen weekly subsidies of $185 each. It was hoped that this would lead to a Canada Council grant.

Early in 1967 Mannering assembled distinctly Canadian fare for an island schools tour, introducing five Canadian writers' works and views of history to secondary schools in Duncan, Chemainus, Nanaimo, Courtenay, Comox, and Sooke. Highlighted was Lister Sinclair's early Scots settlers' play, *The Blood is Strong*, Felix Antoine Savard's *La Salle des Morts, Riel* by John Coulter, and readings from Emily Carr and Vancouver humourist Eric Nichol. This was an excellent political move that also represented both official languages.

It was also during this spring season that Victorians first encountered a young man who was to play a major role in Bastion Theatre's future. He was Edwin Stephenson and he came from Toronto with another Easterner, Dan MacDonald. They were to appear in April's major production.

Meanwhile, Bastion had scored with an almost unbroken line of successes in children's theatre, beginning with its early *Alice in Wonderland* in which a talented, blonde sub-teen named Wendy Packard played the title role. Wendy was the daughter of one of the city's best known and singers, dramatic soprano Peggy Walton Packard. Wendy grew up to be an accomplished dancer and teacher of dance and later married Canadian conductor, Timothy Vernon.

---

[1] Sabiston's highly touted musical, *Napoleon*, opened in Toronto in the fall of 1994. (ed.)

In the fall of 1967 Bastion again drew a blank refusal from Canada Council on its latest request for a grant of $25,000. This persistent rejection ignited a fiery response from Mayor Hugh Stephen. In a telegram to Prime Minister Lester B. Pearson, Stephen referred scathingly to the Council's apparent sympathy towards supporting *avant-garde* art as opposed to "the progressively and culturally stimulating work done by what has grown to be virtually Victoria's civic theatre. What must this civic-minded culturally advanced group do to receive the financial help necessary to its survival?" he demanded.

Three provisos for granting, in addition to growth in audience, had previously been set down by Canada Council. These were, first, a provincial grant, second, a city grant, and third, a professional association. At almost the same time Council's latest refusal was delivered, Bastion had received its first grant under BC's new cultural assistance programme and was also receiving regular financial support from Victoria and from Oak Bay. In addition, Bastion was entering its 1967-68 season as an Equity company. A new undertaking was a course in theatrical design taught by Jack Trueman, the McPherson Playhouse's head lighting designer. The school teaching staff had also been enlarged with the addition of Kay Howard, formerly with CBC radio and the National Film Board, and who was experienced in working with children.

The season's highlight, Shakespeare's *The Taming of the Shrew,* was mounted in January. The cast was headed by Anthony Jenkins of the University of Victoria's English Department and visiting professionals Don McManus and Karen Austin. January was also the month that Canada Council finally came through with a grant of $2,826 — with terms attached. The grant was to be used to allow Joy Coghill of the Vancouver Playhouse Company to direct a play for Bastion and to bring Tibor Feheregyhazi of the Royal Winnipeg Ballet to Victoria as temporary production organizer. As it turned out, however, Coghill was too busy with her own work and Feheregyhazi would be on tour with the ballet until the end of Bastion's season.

Manager Helen Simpson-Baikie was informed that the Canada Council, while offering help in direction and administration, would not provide grants for development of the theatre until the project was self-sustaining within the community. In early spring Bastion received a grant of $7,500 from the new Provincial Centennial Cultural Fund. At Bastion's suggestion the Coghill grant was transferred to Vancouver's Peter Brockington to direct the end-of-season production of *The Innocents*, an adaptation of Henry James's chilling tale, *The Turn of the Screw.*

Only a week before the play's opening, Council's "professional association" dictum brought about a serious loss for Bastion when Canadian Actors' Equity enforced its rule that a company could not be a mixture of paid and unpaid personnel, except for an occasional guest performer. Bastion's headline singer-actor Don McManus, who was also manager and musical director for the company, was forced by this rule to remove himself from the Bastion company.

At this time city planner Rod Clack's renewal programme for Bastion Square was virtually complete and the city was looking for ways to bring people to this area. It was Clack who had suggested to Mannering that his fledgling theatre company should adopt the name Bastion with a view to moving into the old courthouse when work on the square was completed, an idea enthusiastically accepted by Mannering. As plans for the sixth season were made public it became clear that audiences preferred a full roster of plays at the McPherson to a division of production between the Mac and an intimate courthouse theatre. Since it was impractical for Bastion to attempt to accommodate two major programs in separate locations it was decided to adopt the courthouse as a unique classroom site.

In May of that year Bastion finally moved its business office and the school from a Blanshard Street premises opposite Memorial Arena to Bastion Square, the business office being installed on the ground floor (sharing space with the Maritime Museum), while three flights up the theatre school settled into the old courtroom. At this time the technical arm was housed on Henry Street, across Johnson Street Bridge.

In December Bastion endowed its actors with the gift of flight, their holiday production being *Peter Pan*. For this world-renowned expert in stage flight, Peter Foy, was brought to Victoria with all his special equipment. At that time he had four Peter Pans flying about stages in the United States and Canada. Among his flying students had been Mary Martin, Mia Farrow, Johnny Carson, and Carol Burnett.

Altogether it was a big season. Sam Payne directed a full-scale production of Shaw's *Caesar and Cleopatra* for which Roman armour was borrowed from the Stratford Festival. Bastion's children's theatre delighted its audiences with lively versions of fairy tales, including a musical rendering of *Rumpelstiltskin* starring Jerry Gosley, initiator and producer of the popular Victoria summer highlight, *The Smile Show.* The 1969-70 touring programme included *Pinocchio* and a production that, through scenes from *The Threepenny Opera* (Brecht/Weill), and its eighteenth-century prototype, *The Beggar's Opera* (John Gay) traced satire in music through three centuries.

As the 1970s opened there was still no indication that major grants could be expected from Canada Council. The city continued to provide an annual amount of something in excess of $9,000, and assistance also came from the Koerner Foundation, but Bastion was still walking a narrow beam.

Some financial help arrived as summer drew to a close when a grant-in-aid of $3,500 was made by BC Cultural Fund and Canada Council made a one-time grant to allow Toronto's Edwin Stephenson to direct two shows for Bastion. The rationale for these grants was to free Mannering for the adaptation and direction of the company's school tours. These tours were seen as of major importance in terms of their content and the areas covered, which included island communities as far away as Gold River, Ucluelet, Sayward, and Tahsis, in addition to Washington State, the Okanagan, the Kootenays and the Greater Victoria area. That year the tours provided 135 performances.

Despite the general success of the school's touring operation Bastion's struggle to stay alive as the city's chief civic theatre was experiencing increasing difficulties in financing shows that the public wanted to see at prices they were willing and, in many instances able, to pay.

In the spring of 1971 the City Council finance committee heard an urgent plea from Mannering for additional funds to mount the kind of plays the public most wanted to see. With typical evasive action the vote was in favour of Mayor Courtney Haddock's suggestion that "all theatre groups be invited to talk the situation over and see where we are going." More to the point, however, was Alderman Peter Pollen's comment that the city would be the loser if Bastion was forced to discontinue because of a fund shortage.

"We have collected well over $60,000 in rent from Bastion Theatre over the past six years," Pollen pointed out. "Grants at the same time have amounted to about $30,000. It's actually quite a good investment." Aldermen Percy Frampton and Robert Baird also spoke in favour of additional funds for Bastion.

A life-saving announcement by Canada Council was made in June when they endorsed a grant of $14,000 to allow Edwin Stephenson to join the company in December and to direct an Equity season of productions for 1971-72. At the same time Colin Gorrie would come on staff in the late summer to work with Simpson-Baikie in areas of management and would also direct Bastion Theatre School and Workshop productions. Artistic director Mannering would be able to expand the activities of Bastion's highly successful school touring company and children's theatre while continuing to co-ordinate all facets of Bastion's program. With Council supporting these changes Bastion Theatre was finally established alongside Vancouver's Playhouse as one of Canada's fully professional theatres.

December saw advance season ticket sales soar to almost double those of the previous year. The "new look" season under Stephenson's direction opened with a production of the musical *Once Upon a Mattress* with other plays on the agenda including Neil Simon's *Plaza Suite* and Peter Shaffer's *Five Finger Exercise*. Another bright spot as the year drew to a close was the success of the Mannering touring company which had given seventy-two performances of a musical version of *Cinderella* for elementary students and an adaptation of *The Importance of Being Earnest* for secondary schools. The successful McPherson Playhouse season under Stephenson drew overall favourable reviews and much-improved houses.

Funding swelled further in 1972 when Bastion's new studio company, directed jointly by Colin and his wife, Elizabeth, was awarded a federal grant of $20,845 under the Local Initiatives Program (LIP). Altogether the season concluded on an optimistic level — audiences had doubled, reviews were generally good, and the Canada Council had announced a $20,000 grant for the forthcoming season. There was a demand for longer runs of the main stage productions and the pre-sale of season tickets was encouraging. The Gorries' studio theatre was working creatively using interesting and original material and Mannering's touring company, after a successful season that covered 3,374 miles with 28 performances to 55,000 youngsters, was home and already looking forward to its tenth year. Honorary citizenships were conferred on Mannering and Helen Simpson-Baikie in January of 1973 in recognition of their valuable work in the community.

A Canadian playwright and professional Victoria actors became prominent in 1973. *The Killdeer*, a sensitive play by James Reaney, brought singer-actor Don McManus back to the city to head a cast that included Margaret Martin, John Heath, and Victoria Theatre Guild's Phyllis Gaskell and Dorothea House. This production was a significant success on many artistic levels as well as with the audiences. At the same time the children's theatre came on strongly with *The Thirteen Clocks*, a fairy story by James Thurber embellished with music. This production was directed by Sylvia Hosie and featured Ian McIntyre, who had been an outstanding student talent with Mannering's earlier school. McIntyre later became a busy professional actor based in Toronto but continued to be seen from time to time in Bastion roles.

A slowdown hit the economy in the winter of 1973 and municipal budget cutting was experienced. Inevitably the arts were

136

among the first to be lopped, being regarded as nice if you can afford them, but nonessential if you can't. Major arts organizations were the targets of Saanich's axe-wielding — Bastion Theatre was cut back to its 1972 level, an increase to the Art Gallery of Greater Victoria was denied, and the Conservatory of Music's request was turned down altogether. In midsummer Canada Council, however, announced its new grant to Bastion Theatre would be $30,000, ten thousand more than Bastion had received in the previous year.

Bastion personnel were on the move in the late spring. Stephenson was in the east both acting and directing as well as carrying on discussions regarding a Bastion/Theatre New Brunswick interchange and meeting with representatives of Canada Council concerning projections and grants. Mannering was in England and Scotland touring children's theatre and returned to Victoria with a case full of plays and masses of notes accumulated on a Canada Council-sponsored study tour.

Stephenson confirmed that Theatre New Brunswick would bring *Death of a Salesman* to Victoria while Bastion's successful production of the irresistible comedy *Born Yesterday* would travel to New Brunswick. While in Ottawa performing in *Mrs. Warren's Profession* Stephenson had commented, in an interview with the Ottawa *Citizen*, that a disturbing factor in Victoria's civic theatre situation was that while the Bastion Theatre Company would be paying almost $19,000 rent for the city-owned McPherson Playhouse in the coming year, the city's grant to Bastion was only $4,000. Whether or not the publicized comment on the obvious inequality had any effect with City Council, notice was taken by the province. In October of that year BC's annual cultural grant to Bastion was $38,500, the largest of all Victoria-area arts organizations.

Further highlights of the 1970s included a third move of Bastion's office and support areas from the courthouse to the Malahat Building on Wharf Street. Apart from its harbour view this proved anything but satisfactory as the space allotted was inadequate. The need for facilities for rehearsing, children's classes, costume storage and construction, and a dozen other services was shrugged aside.

However, such was the success of the theatre school activity that at the start of its twelfth season the five-play children's theatre programme moved into its own intimate theatre on lower Yates Street. In addition young audience members could, for the first time, purchase their own season tickets. School tours continued to be popular, reaching ever further afield with requests for visits as far as Dawson Creek in northern BC and from the Gulf Islands. Links were also forged with the Victoria Conservatory of Music and with the advanced theatre school created at Camosun College under Maurice Harty. An attic space in a lower Yates Street building had been acquired for Bastion's rehearsals and theatre school classes and was shared with Camosun students.

The 1976-77 season would celebrate the fifth year for Bastion as a fully professional theatre. The roster of plays included Anthony Shaffer's thriller *Sleuth,* imported from the Vancouver Arts Club, George S. Kaufman's *The Man Who Came to Dinner,* Coward's *Present Laughter,* Shaw's *Saint Joan,* and Anouilh's *Ring Round the Moon.* The previous season had amassed 4,000 subscribers and the goal was to boost that number by 500.

Bastion now had 150 employees, an annual budget of more than $390,000, and a per-capita subscription rate that was impressive. It also had the satisfaction of having stuck to its guns by refusing to abandon children's theatre when Canada Council suggested it be dropped so that resources could be concentrated on mainstage production. The directors' philosophy held that continuing survival of the theatre depended to a considerable extent on the induction of new generations into early contact with the living stage.

A Canada Council grant of $105,000 and a promise of the same amount in the following year brought visions of further growth. In the meantime the eastern Canada press was becoming inquisitive, references often being made to "Bastion Theatre of Canada." Staff was expanded to cover all aspects of the theatre's operation. Glynis Leyshon took over public relations and John Heath was put under contract in a first step towards establishing a resident company. His initial assignment was to direct, design, and choreograph the season opener, *Godspell.* At this point Stephenson had no regrets over having turned a deaf ear to Toronto doomsayers who had warned him against coming to Victoria.

In the fall of 1976 Bastion was invited to open the season for the English theatre section of the National Arts Centre in Ottawa. Stephenson chose Georges Feydeau's virtuoso farce, *A Stitch in Time,* a tissue of hysterical and sexy nonsense that has nevertheless survived almost a century. The sets, cases of properties, and costumes set off for Ottawa on a foray masterminded with great success by Ian Poole, a young man who had learned the art of going on the road as a result of several seasons of touring with Bastion's youth company. Another Feydeau farce, *A Flea in Her Ear,* opened the 1980s and individual ticket sales soared past the $50,000 mark. Sadly characteristic of response to Canadian plays, John Murrell's *Waiting for the Parade* followed, generating no heat at the box office, and then for Christmas, one more time — *Life With Father.* This production was staged by associate director Ron Ulrich and was a runaway success. It was also the first Bastion production to have joint sponsorship of two major Canadian corporations — Shell Canada and IBM Canada. All previous records fell as the Bastion chalked up theatre capacities over 90% for some performances. Box office sales amounted to an astonishing $54,900 and recorded 6,201 subscribers.

A landmark undertaking that involved a huge cast was *Richard III.* It required the collaboration of Camosun College theatre students in addition to notable Canadian actors Irene Mayeska, Peter Brockington, Susan Chapple, and Jim McQueen in major roles. The handsome set and costumes earned high praise for young Victoria designer, the late Jack Simon, and also for the dramatic effectiveness of Jack Trueman's intelligent lighting.

Both press and public were enthusiastic and Canada Council's visiting representative, David Peacock (who attended the opening) described the production as "highly effective." This was the season when Council awarded Bastion Theatre one of the highest grant increases given to any theatre company in Canada. The production of *Richard III* broke all attendance records up to that time and there was a 60% increase in subscribers over the previous season with average attendance soaring to over 75% of capacity.

Expectations among Bastion Theatre's staff and board of directors were high that the first production of the eighties, *Deathtrap*, would be another record-smasher. This play was a thriller that was, at the time, filling theatres on both sides of the Atlantic. The fact that Bastion had acquired Canada's greatest internationally acclaimed actor, Douglas Rain, for the lead was also positive. Stephenson had scooped everyone by making Bastion the first North American theatre outside Broadway to acquire the stock company rights to *Deathtrap*. He directed, noted Canadian designer Ed Kotanen returned to create sets and costumes, and Jack Trueman created the lighting. Co-sponsors were the *Times*, the *Colonist*, and Westcoast Savings and Credit Union.

The expectations were fulfilled. *Deathtrap* did, indeed, eclipse the holiday show record. Attendance was up more than 10%, reaching a total of 11,345 and box office receipts totalled $57,500. Earned revenues for the season, with two productions still to come, amounted to $199,250. General manager Eric Macdonald optimistically contemplated the complete season revenues would pass the $300,000 mark. Total attendance for that season's mainstage and youth tour surpassed $125,000. In addition Bastion had launched a high-powered fund-raising campaign. The objective over three years was to raise $500,000, largely for operating capital. Co-chairs working with general manager Macdonald were Maryla Waters, at that time president of the board, and board member Michael Field.

At the opening performance of 1980-81 season, Lieutenant Governor Henry Bell-Irving announced that henceforth the company would be known officially as the Bastion Theatre Company of British Columbia. In keeping with that announcement, a further reach than ever before was undertaken when Stephenson led a tour of the mainstage production of *The Importance of Being Earnest* to various interior communities, while the Youth Tour played to more than 85,000 school children. Specific fund-raisers of the eighties included such substantial efforts as two highly successful dinner auctions, the Chocolate Festival in 1985, and the Expo '88 travel raffle with a myriad of associated events.

For 1980-81 Bastion planned a tenth professional anniversary season which was to include a number of special fund-raising ventures. *The Miracle Worker* was scheduled as the October opener. Assisted by the Deaf and Hard of Hearing Institute of Vancouver Island, Bastion, with the co-operation of the McPherson Playhouse, presented its first "signed" performance with interpreter Fran Odinsky. Since that time the McPherson management has installed a system of hearing aids for those patrons requiring them.

A welcome gift marking the Christmas season of 1981 was an endowment fund cheque for $25,000 from IBM, but the year also marked the beginning of a downswing in the economy. This was also the year of Edwin Stephenson's departure as artistic director. He had made an outstanding contribution to the quality and stamina of Bastion Theatre but felt it was time to seek a new challenge and a different venue. The financial drought was worsening and audiences were falling well below the high water mark of the seventies in which season subscribers had reached nearly seven thousand. The Bastion board's choice as replacement for Ed was Keith Digby who was then working with John Neville, the noted British actor-director who was artistic director of Edmonton's Citadel Theatre. Digby had also been artistic director of Theatre 3, Edmonton's alternate theatre.

In shaping his perception for Bastion Digby emphasized high impact, theatricality, freshness, and an appetizing blend of popular theatre with a connoisseur sampling of new works plus an occasional embellishment of classics. The season opened with Shakespeare's *A Midsummer Night's Dream.* The production included spectacular sets and costumes, imaginative lighting, and originality in placing the fairytale play in a rustic area of Victoria in the mid-Victorian age. The nobles were turned into officers from a visiting British frigate and the "mechanicals" into below-deck sailors — altogether a lively and refreshing concept.

The second half of his first season contained another outstanding production among the several that were memorable in Digby's six seasons with the company, *The Gin Game* by D. L. Coburn. This two-character play and Pulitzer Prize winner had been the hit of the season in New York where it had starred the brilliant husband-and-wife team, Jessica Tandy and Hume Cronyn. For Bastion Digby had obtained an outstanding team in Canadian actors Ann Casson and Wally McSween. This well-staged production was vivid, polished, and touching, as well as wildly comic. It was a deserved triumph but not received entirely without reproof from a few elder audience members, much disturbed at the realism of certain scenes in which the language became heated to the point of "tastelessness," according to one elderly gentlemen who phoned to rebuke me for giving such a show "a four-star rating" in my review.

Two other memorable productions before the season's end were the medieval-historical *The Lion in Winter* and Joe Orton's wild comedy *What the Butler Saw*. These excellent theatre works revealed, among other things, Digby's talent for casting and for perception in choosing the right director for the vehicle. Among its audiences some tut-tutting went on regarding language in the Orton play, but Vancouver reviewers who came over for the "new-look" season found it not daring but conformist!

While Digby lined up his second season Bastion's board found itself in a deficit situation, due more than anything to the severity of the economic slump on Vancouver Island. Season ticket holders dropped within three years from 6,000 to 4,500. While that problem might have been endured the recession had also greatly diminished single ticket sales for both professional theatres, Bastion and Belfry. The Bastion Youth Tour was also feeling the stress from reductions in education funding, but its current show, *Superwheel,* about the relationships adolescents have with their cars, was bright, breezy and tuneful and caught on with its high school audiences. Not only the students received it well, but school officials were enthusiastic and the RCMP and Victoria police were interested in possible involvement of the show in the education of young drivers.

Undiscouraged by the economic retrenchment, Digby set as one of his goals winning back as many as possible of the 1,500 subscribers who had dropped away. With this in view, he opened with Shaw's *Candida*, a rare import from the Niagara-on-the-Lake Shaw Festival. The season was to contain further memorable selections. The first of these was former CBC staff writer Suzanne Finlay's first stage play, *Monkeyshines*, which starred Canada's irresistible actress, Frances Hyland, and Michael Ball. The two were a finely honed duo in a gentle, whimsical concoction. Balance was given to the season by the inclusion of Canadian playwright Sharon Pollock's tensely dramatic *Blood Relations*, based on a real-life multiple murder — the Lizzie Borden story. In strong relief there was actor-writer Warren Graves' *Scrooge* at Christmas. Digby's well-chosen season proved an outstanding success that resulted by mid-April in 2,200 of the targeted 4,000 subscribers being already signed up for the 1984-85 season.

However, the Bastion's accumulated deficit had reached $265,000 in an overall budget of $1.1 million and the problem had become critical. Faced with the most serious crisis in Bastion history the board took a step that at the time appeared to initiate a major financial move in the development of professional Canadian theatre. In the spring of 1984 the board of directors announced a $500,000 issue of sinking fund debentures. It was anticipated investors would buy the bonds which would produce higher interest than the current bank savings rates. Bastion would then not only be able to pay off its deficit but have in excess of $200,000 to invest at seven per cent compound interest, doubling itself in 10 years, thus protecting the investors' money. Additionally, investors would be able to use the fund as a tax write-off. Echoes that the plan would be imitated by other Canadian cultural organizations came from many sources. Commented board chairman Peter Bennett, "It will be nice to be imitated but it's even nicer to be first."

Once the plan was approved by the BC Securities Commission, similar schemes were being considered in Vancouver and other BC cities. Digby commented in the *Globe and Mail*: "It's about time arts groups direct some of their creative energy toward creative financing. It will stop people thinking that arts groups are all run by flaky people!"

This innovative concept, however, was not the success that had been anticipated. Purchase of the debentures stalled at around $50,000. Many people approached said they would rather give Bastion an outright donation. Eventually a more modest fund was established with the Vancouver Foundation making a matching grant to the IBM grant of $25,000.

The artistic quality of the 1987-88 season, however, was outstanding. One fine production that brought the public thronging to the McPherson during this period was Harold Pinter's *Betrayal.* Undoubtedly a pinnacle among the range of Bastion's productions was the impressively mounted and performed musical, *Sweeney Todd, The Demon Barber of Fleet Street.* In it Margaret Martin played the diabolical Mrs. Lovett, cohort of "demon barber" Todd. The title role was played by Stratford Festival star Graeme Campbell, noted for his Bill Sykes in Broadway's *Oliver.* Included in the large cast of principals was tenor Richard Margison. To close the season a colourfully bizarre presentation of Sheridan's *School for Scandal* was mounted in collaboration with the Vancouver Playhouse. The six-play season saw three of the plays achieve 6,000 in ticket sales. Keith Digby departed as artistic director at the end of that season and nobody could have guessed that the end of the road was in sight.

The 25th anniversary season (1988-89) with new artistic director Barry McGregor began on schedule to a background chorus of encomiums from all sources, beginning with Canada Council's statement that the Bastion was "a strongly ongoing and developing artistic organization." Artistic value and success was highlighted in reviews by local, mainland, and up-island critics as well as business executives of companies that were financial contributors. Then, without warning, in the middle of the anniversary season and in the presence of a summoned audience of media representatives, the final curtain was lowered on the twenty-five-year-old Bastion.

Shock was manifest and questions erupted — what had caused this unexpected and unwelcome turn of events? What, if any, action could be taken to undo the catastrophe? Escalating rental at the McPherson was named the principal villain.

At its inception the McPherson Foundation agreed that keeping the theatre rental at a level manageable to local organizations was a prime consideration. It was inevitable, however, that costs for operating the theatre would rise. If that did not, then maintaining the theatre and added improvements such as wheelchair access and hard-of-hearing assistance would be impossible. While the McPherson had begun its rebirth and carried on for some time as a non-union house with a loyal and excellent front-of-house and backstage staff, it was inevitable that this situation could not be permanent, especially once the long-unionized Royal was brought under the management of the McPherson Foundation.

Everyone was seeking a villain. Actually, no one circumstance, no one individual or group could be identified. There had been errors of judgement, unexpected costs, and unanticipated failures at the box office that levelled off the big successes such as *Sweeney Todd* and *Life with Father*. There was no Bastion Foundation like the Victoria Symphony Foundation which had been established to cope with sudden stress situations. So at age 25 an industry that had attracted hundreds of thousands of dollars a year into the city, died. It is ironic that most of its $1 million yearly was spent within the city on wages for local residents, crafts persons, and technicians, as well as on supplies from local dealers. It is also notable that the McPherson Playhouse was deeper in "the red" after Bastion's demise than before.

Eventually, in 1990, a New Bastion appeared, more modest in its reach, avoiding big-ticket productions, and without the highly desirable but costly appendages of a school and youth touring company. The New Bastion, rising out of the ashes of its celebrated forerunner, has mounted shortened seasons of judiciously selected low-profile plays at the McPherson. Unfortunately, as the 1990s decade move forward so does a deep-biting recession that has closed down, or diminished to a trickle, not only grant resources on a large scale, but also lists of patrons, benefactors, and donors.

CHAPTER FIFTEEN

The Phoenix

*E*LSEWHERE in the city promising initiatives were developing. Victoria College had, since its establishment, provided two introductory years for students heading for the University of British Columbia or other institutions of higher learning. In 1963 it became the full-fledged University of Victoria and its focus, in the view of first president Malcolm Taylor, was to become a fine arts university in addition to offering degrees in psychology, history, and philosophy. A theatre department and a music school were to be established immediately.

Victoria College had been housed at one time in Craigdarroch Castle but in 1946 the college was moved into the former teacher-training centre (the Provincial Normal School) on Lansdowne Road This accommodation was obviously too limited for the development of a comprehensive degree-granting university. While awaiting permanent construction on the new university site at Gordon Head a great deal more space was required.

During the war years at Gordon Head many acres of what had been farm land were turned into a military camp with numerous hutments for the accommodation of army units, their offices, and support services. This area was vacated some time after the war's end and in 1961 was designated as the location of the new university campus. Hutments were moved, extended, and transformed into makeshift classrooms and labs and the new university's student body divided its time between the "Lansdowne" campus and the "Gordon Head" campus.

Almost from the beginning there had been a theatre presence at Victoria College, encouraged by English professor Roger Bishop.

With a view to future development he steered the active College Players Club to salt away its earnings from its usually profitable productions. When, in 1961, it seemed that his vision might become a reality, Bishop was informed that certain army huts were to be made available for a campus theatre.

Classics professor and UVIC historian Dr. Peter Smith soon joined forces with Bishop in urging the development of theatre on the campus. They had their sights set on enticing back to Victoria Carl Hare, a young professor of English who had earlier taught at Victoria College. Hare was born in Edmonton, was a gold medallist in English with an Honours BA and diploma from the Royal Academy of Dramatic Art. At the time Hare was doing radio and television shows as well as stage plays in Vancouver. He had no intention of going back to university teaching but when Bishop told him of the new campus theatre plan the temptation for him and his creative wife, Clara, was strong. They returned to Victoria and both were to have a lasting impact upon theatre in Victoria.

A young Vancouver designer was hired to produce a set of plans for the new "complex" using the proceeds of a production of *Othello* done by the English department the year before. His raw materials were a group of abandoned army huts and the outcome was the development of the original Phoenix. Much was accomplished in this theatre-in-a-hut by those Victorians for whom "going to the Phoenix" was not just the "in-thing" but a much enjoyed and long-lasting experience.

Q hut was a small space in which not-so-small miracles took place. Here the Campus Players, composed of UVIC faculty and wives, staff and students, and non-UVIC persons was formed. It was truly a town-and-gown company. Creativity abounded and proved — as Carl was again to demonstrate — that wonderful effects could be achieved when lack of funds challenged inventive use of whatever came to hand. Choice of plays ranged widely from Euripides' *The Bacchae* and across the centuries to Shakespeare's *Twelfth Night*, Chekov's *The Three Sisters*, O'Neill's *A Long Days Journey into Night*, and Robert Bolt's *A Man for All Seasons*, among others.

Even before the full development of the site Hare produced a spirited version of *The Alchemist* in a beautifully-paced presentation. Notable cast members included English professors Anthony Jenkins and Michael Warren, as well as Victoria lawyer Foster Isherwood, and students Christopher Ross (grandson of Jenny Butchart who created the famous Gardens), Bob Chamut, Pat Scott, and Dougal Fraser. Hare and Smith again collaborated in 1966 in a town-and-gown production of *The Braggart Warrior* by the Roman playwright Plautus. The cast included talented Victorians Helen Smith and Margaret Hall, Robert Price, and Dougal Fraser. Fraser was greatly praised in the title role of this classic and later won admission to, and subsequently graduated from, London's Royal Academy of Dramatic Art and has pursued a successful career on stage.

In their production of *The Birds*, the amount of assembled talent at UVIC was clearly demonstrated. In addition to being locally cast, the work was adapted from the Greek of Aristophanes by Peter Smith with incidental music composed by Dr. Chet Lambertson of the English Department. This was a complete and much talked-about success among Victoria theatre-goers.

The dawn of the 1970s marked a decade of both growth and upheaval in the UVIC Theatre Department. Carl Hare had been called upon more than once to convert his acting chairmanship of the theatre division into a permanent situation. His basic interest, however, lay less with administration than it did in directing, acting, and teaching. He was impatient to return to the creative aspect, so UVIC embarked on a search for a theatre department head. The person chosen was an authority on theatre history, having co-authored with John Gassner *Theatre and Drama in the Making* (1964), considered a major reference work in the field. Dr. Ralph Allen was, at the time of accepting the directorship of the UVIC theatre department, head of theatre at the University of Pittsburgh. What was it that lured him to Victoria? With his academic standing among United States' universities, why did he come to the west coast of Canada to a brand-new university that had barely had time to make itself known in its own country, let alone in the United States?

When Dr. Allen visited UVIC in the summer of 1968 I sought an interview with him. Over lunch he was quite open about his intentions in taking up residence in Victoria. The principal lure had been the presence in the city of its fully restored theatre, the McPherson Playhouse.

"I'm planning to start a summer festival here; this city is an ideal spot for what could become a Stratford Festival of the west," he told me. I could only applaud this thought and hope that he had the magic to bring it about. He also remarked that theatre students should not spend a lot of time in the classroom, but could best learn by doing.

True enough. Still, as with most performing arts, there is much beyond the actual "hands on" application that needs to be researched and understood. This can only be absorbed and utilized with hours of study, reading, and listening.

Dr. Allen arrived with his wife, Harriet, in September. He brought with him a quite extraordinary artist, Robert Cothran. Tall, soft-spoken, and often seeming to be lost in thought, he was a master of design. Much of his work with what would become Victoria Fair would eclipse anything that had gone before in this city.

Victoria Fair — everyone involved wished to avoid the word "festival" — became a reality at the McPherson Playhouse in the summer of 1969. It was established, on a repertory basis, with Shakespeare's plays *Hamlet* and *The Merchant of Venice* and Molière's *Tartuffe* being performed alternately throughout the six weeks of summer. For virtually the first time theatre critics from distant places began to look west, alert to what was happening in this far-off tourist and retirement haven on the Pacific coast. *Saturday Review's* critic Henry Hewes had softly glowing praise for the performance values of *Tartuffe*, but he and others were stirred into seeking fresh plaudits for the set designs of Cothran. They were exquisite in decor, authentic as to period in every detail of style and colour, and as well, the furnishings and hand props were meticulously selected or specially made to harmonize with the *mise en scène*.

The University of Victoria's School of Music faculty, with occasional guests, also contributed musical programs as part of Victoria

Fair. The concerts, including solo and chamber performances, took place in the MacLaurin building lecture hall (now the David Lam Auditorium) which was used for musical events before the fine Philip T. Young Recital Hall and University Centre Auditorium were built. These concerts were funded, in part, by Canada Council grants, as was the Victoria Fair theatre program. Whether or not these grants would have continued or for how long is difficult to conjecture. Probably not indefinitely unless there had been some prospect of civic input for the costly downtown presentations. Even taking into account Canada Council assistance the drain on the University's funding for the theatre department was considerable and as time went by caused some concern across campus.

Much sought-after experts in various fields of theatre had been appointed to UVIC theatre in previous months. Among the first to join the faculty were Will and Jane Benson, an English family. Will was a swordsman who had coached many actors on the English stage and Jane was a voice coach. Their daughter Susan, a teenager at the time, possessed exceptional talent in costume design and intended to enter that profession as soon as her schooling was finished. They remained at UVIC for only a short time, feeling that their talents were being under used, especially with respect to Victoria Fair. As a result of this disenchantment the family soon moved to Ontario where they were quickly acquired by the Stratford Festival. Susan was to steadily develop her special genius and is recognized today as one of the leading costume designers in Canada.

Britain and Japan are two countries particularly noted for the development of children's theatre. In Britain a strong lead had been taken in the use of theatre as a tool in education. Largely through the innovative powers and teaching personality of Richard Courtney the creation of techniques in the use of children's theatre as a developmental tool for youngsters of varying ages and mental capacities was established in a diploma course at London University. In the course of time Courtney's exceptional ability and the importance of his subject was recognized internationally. He was invited to Acadia

University in Nova Scotia to initiate programs and lecture on the subject.

When he was ready to move on, other Canadian universities were beckoning. With the University of Calgary and the University of Victoria competing for him he finally chose Victoria and moved here with his wife and family in 1968.

Courtney's requirements on UVIC's space and finances were modest in the extreme. His view of children's theatre calls upon and encourages development and expansion of that special aspect of childhood — imagination. It encourages a search for everyday materials — a length of cord that can become Eve's serpent, a scrap of paper that will metamorphose into a bird, and balloons that offer endless possibilities. He considers the use of these and other common materials as important tools in creative play. Potential teachers learn to adapt and to see how and where to adapt. They learn to interact with others, to explore and experiment and gain knowledge of the world around them as seen by the very young. Most of Courtney's students had teaching as a goal. They were enthusiastic and dedicated, absorbed in discovering exciting possibilities in simple things, in learning how to stretch a child's imagination, and how to manipulate and open doors to expand the growing mind rather than hedge it in with formulæ.

In spite of his modest demands, Courtney soon discovered that neither his ideas nor the aspirations he had for his students were receiving much support from the increasingly production-oriented theatre department. He took what he saw as the only possible dignified course available to him by submitting his resignation. Ralph Allen expressed regret at Courtney's departure but asserted that the department had no intention of relinquishing developmental drama and that he was determined to find the best person possible to replace Courtney. Courtney went on to become a senior member of faculty at the University of Calgary and later at the Ontario Institute for Studies in Education, the graduate school of education at the University of Toronto.

With the departure of the Bensons and Courtney questions began to arise, particularly among those from the community who had had a close association with the Campus Players. At the centre of the controversy was the apparent focus of the Department on the mounting of Victoria Fair's handsome and lavish showpieces at a downtown theatre at the perceived expense of the academic development of the Department.

Since I was made very much aware of the situation from both on- and off-campus sources at the time, one of my regular *Times* columns posed the question: "Can UVIC Afford Victoria Fair?" The article focused on the general perception that student-oriented activities in the Theatre Department seemed to be taking a back seat to what many considered to be its non-academic pursuits. I was careful to point out, however, that there is a distinct advantage for theatre students to being able to view and work in professional productions from time to time. I also made it clear that both the Canada Council, the university, and certain individuals had committed funds to the project but that neither downtown business nor City Hall made any contribution while enjoying wide publicity and fat rentals.

On an evening following these events the latest production destined for Victoria Fair 1971 was given a preview at the McPherson. This was in the nature of a special fund-raiser for an excursion to Ottawa where the play was to be the Victoria entrant in the Canadian Drama Festival, the successor to the Dominion Drama Festival. The play, a tragedy by sixteenth-century Spanish playwright Lope de Vaga, was *Justice Not Revenge*. When I arrived to cover the opening for the *Times*, outside the theatre a congregation of students had a surprise for me. They were giving out yellow flyers to all comers. Printed on them was the full text of my column and inside the theatre foyer was one young woman distributing copies of Allen's three-column page-length ad which he had purchased in answer to my article.

A highlight of his response was that I could have found the answers to my rhetorical questions if I had troubled to phone either Dean Garvie or himself. The fact was that cordial relations, or contact of any kind, between Allen, Garvie, and myself had ceased the day my critical review of Allen's production of *The Duchess of Malfi* appeared. My general view had been that the principal flaws in a visually handsome production were its general lack of powerful rhythm and shaping, without which such a dark tragedy becomes laboured. There was excellent talent and capability among the large cast but these elements had not been forged into the compelling experience that hypnotizes an audience. There were several aspects that were highly commendable and to which my subsequent review drew attention. There could be no avoiding, however, the overall lack of dramatic impact or the frequently unclear speech.

Diction was a real problem in the *Malfi* performance. People going up the aisles at intermission and discussing the performance in the foyer were asking each other if they had understood what the actors were saying. Having also had some difficulty in this area, I could sympathize. During the several years I had spent directing for the Theatre Guild I had discovered that one tends to become so familiar with the text that instinctively when an actor fumbles his lines the director can give the prompt without a script in hand. It is still my belief that Allen needed someone in the auditorium during final rehearsals — a sit-in, shall we say — who was not familiar with the text and could sound a warning.

From the day of my review of *Malfi* cordiality between myself, Dean Garvie, Allen, and their associates ended. We never spoke again until we played out our own little drama of the absurd. The night after my review of *Malfi* was published I attended a concert which was part of Victoria Fair in the University's MacLaurin Building. The Dean and I met head on in the hall. I had a smile of greeting poised on my face but it never got any further. He walked by, looking straight through me. At the intermission Allen and his group kept their distance. From that point the formally friendly birds-of-a-feather dialogue, initiated in the first place by Doctors Allen and Garvie, ceased. We had become strangers. So they did not like honest criticism, only plaudits. Fine. So be it. The climax to this little drama, however, was to be played out later that fall after Dr. Allen, having lost the University's endorsement of Victoria Fair, announced his return to the United States. His last production was to be the medieval morality play *Everyman* to be staged in the original Phoenix Theatre hut.

In the interim there had been other UVIC Fine Arts events, but no requests for coverage arrived on my desk. At that time of year we were inundated with requests to review a variety of performances and I had no time for nail-biting over the schism between UVIC Fine Arts and myself. One late afternoon in November I was hard at work in an almost empty newsroom when an editor approached with a question: was I intending to review a play at the Phoenix Theatre that evening? No I wasn't — why did he ask? He'd just received a call, he told me, from someone in the UVIC Theatre Department saying they'd heard that if Mrs. Johnson arrived at the Phoenix that evening she would be ordered to leave. The whole thing seemed so incredible that I started to laugh.

"No, I'm not kidding," he said. "The person who phoned was quite serious, so I think you'll have to go."

"What do I do about tickets? They've probably told the box office not to issue me any."

He said that was no problem. "We'll get a reporter to phone the box office and reserve a couple. Come to think of it another reporter had better go with you. Seeing you're central to the story it wouldn't be fair to ask you to write it if you were nursing bruises after being tossed out." It wasn't fair to send me at all, I thought, but such drastic action still seemed highly improbable. After all, these were highly respected academics who would never lower themselves to engaging in gutter-type behaviour.

When I got home I told Maurice the incredible story and he laughed. That's just bluff, was his first reaction. During dinner, having second thoughts, he decided he'd better accompany me. At the time he was a member of the University Senate. We arrived on that chilly November night and stepped through the door into the warm lobby already populated with chatting groups. We had gone no further than six feet before Allen, flanked by two students, confronted us. We were eyeball-to-eyeball for the first time in many weeks.

"Mrs. Johnson," he said formally, "we took a vote today and it was agreed that we do not want you in the theatre, so we're asking you now to leave."

Out of the corner of my eye I could see our male reporter — my bodyguard — collecting the tickets at the box office. With Maurice at my elbow I fixed my eyes on Ralph and said calmly that in these or any similar circumstances the only instruction I took was from my editor, which was in the present instance, to attend this evening's performance.

He then demanded to know how I had procured tickets and when I told him they had been reserved by telephone on behalf of the newsroom his response was "so you got them by underhanded means!" He then demanded to know if I intended to review this production. When I replied in the affirmative, he said, "We don't want your review." To which I responded that what mattered with me was what my editor wanted.

Our dialogue was conducted at a low-key level. No one among the gathering audience was aware of the confrontation. A friend who had noticed us conversing from across the foyer told me afterward he had thought that our differences had been resolved. At this point Dean Garvie entered and was immediately summoned by Allen as reinforcement. To Garvie's somewhat embarrassed endorsement that I should leave, my response again was that the editor's instructions ranked ahead of theirs.

Garvie retired from the fray and Allen turned to his rear guard with the command: "Go and fetch the security police!" Maurice entered the joust at this point with a warning: "Dr. Allen, before any attempt is made to eject my wife from this theatre, I should advise you to consult with the University's solicitors."

Allen put on an act of ignoring the warning. As for me, I felt the tension mount but to tell the truth rather enjoyed being featured in this off-stage melodrama. The situation came to an abrupt end, however, with the arrival of UVIC's public relations officer, Maurice Cownden. On learning what was afoot, Cownden put a sharp period to the episode. He reminded Allen of President Partridge's instruction that there should be an end to public confrontation and also pointed out that Allen had no authority to evict anyone. "This is not your theatre," he said, "it's public property."

After I had seen the production, which was again a visual delight as designed by Cothran, I was joined on leaving the theatre by a friend who was a UVIC professor and a talented actor. He asked me anxiously what I was going to do. I was puzzled. What did he mean? It seemed he failed to understand how I could settle down with an open mind to review the performance after all that had happened in the foyer. I tried to explain that the verbal duel (over in seconds, really) would not affect my ability to be objective concerning what I subsequently had seen on the stage. In fact, if anything, it would make me more aware of the need to dissociate the one from the other.

Allen and I never met again and he and Garvie left Victoria a short time later. Allen's most profound interest and expertise lay in the historical aspect of theatre, specifically in researching and bringing forward long forgotten works of early dramatists. He was a scholar of considerable depth and an authority on the development of theatre through the ages. I had many memorable conversations with Ralph Allen before our relationship soured. One interesting facet I discovered was that his passion for antiquity was balanced by an equal enthusiasm for certain concepts of more recent time such as farce and the burlesque theatre. He was to carry this interest later to the scripting, though not the direction, of a unique Broadway show that marked the amazing return of Mickey Rooney to the New York stage, *Sugar Babies*.

When Ralph Allen left the university in 1972 he was succeeded by Dr. Barbara McIntyre, a specialist in children's theatre. Dr. McIntyre proved to be exactly the right person to turn things around in the department and to re-establish direction. In an interview, Carl Hare commented that "Dr. McIntyre of necessity acted as a poultice — a cure for the department's sense of its wounds. There were serious problems within the department — personality clashes, irreconcilable differences." Dr. McIntyre allowed time for the scars to heal and for animosities and problems to subside and die away.

She was also instrumental in reinstating the Summer Senior Secondary Theatre Workshop for students who attended from all over the province.

During a period in the seventies a government-sponsored Senior Secondary Summer Theatre Workshop reached out across the province and provided training and experience in theatre arts for six weeks on the UVIC campus. The students were involved both on stage and backstage, learning technical skills such as the fine art of lighting and sound production. Under the guidance of a visiting director these students worked on a play chosen for its challenges and in the final week presented it publicly in the Phoenix Theatre. They were introduced to some of the finest plays written in our own time as well those of other centuries. These workshops were discontinued in the early eighties.

When Allen and Robert Cothran returned to the States, Victoria was by no means left barren in the realm of theatre design. There were on campus some promising youthful talents. Most importantly there was Bill West, a visionary and at the same time a soundly practical and versatile artist with a pervading sense of mood and place. At the time of Cothran's departure West was one of three teachers conducting a secondary school arts programme at Oak Bay. The other two were Carole Sabiston, now an internationally known artist, and Beth Hannigan.

Dr. McIntyre invited West to be scene designer at UVIC's Phoenix and he accepted, not without doubts as to his qualifications in this particular area and regret at leaving his Oak Bay classes. "Nothing can flatter the ego of a teacher like an enthusiastic high school kid," he smilingly reflected on recalling his mixed feelings. However, Dr. McIntyre convinced him and to his outstanding gifts as a teacher were added his particular abilities as a technician, a designer, and an engineer. All of these qualities were to play a vital part in the design of the new Phoenix Building.

The genius of Robert Cothran is probably the element that will be most indelibly imprinted on the minds of those who attended the Victoria Fair series of productions. But in truth, theatre in Victoria since then, especially in the last two decades, has come close to being dominated by the general excellence of the set and costume designers. While Cothran's work was astonishing in its beauty and detail it did tend to be an overwhelming element to the extent of distracting one's eyes and therefore one's mind from the course of the play. During an interview I had with this rather reclusive and unassuming artist he observed that "the best I can do is sometimes the worst I can do." Asked to clarify the comment he replied that while design and decor is desirable to establish place, style, mood, and period, it should never be so distinctive as to distract attention from the play's statement and its interpretation by the actors.

His comment awakened a theatrical memory still vivid after some 20 years. The occasion had been a visit to Victoria by Stratford Festival's short-lived winter road company. The play was Shaw's *Saint Joan*, the place was Victoria High School auditorium. It was touring on a shoestring budget, inevitable for most companies travelling Canada's awesome distances. The tours were planned to keep Stratford Festival's actors engaged between summer sessions. Even so, expenses proved too high and the stripped-down staging was unappealing to many audiences, so the tours were discontinued.

In *Saint Joan* the scenery consisted of dark curtains and risers with the barely adequate essentials of lighting. Costumes were spare and based on symbolism. Clerics wore simple black gowns with wooden crosses on thongs around their necks, soldiers and other characters were similarly symbolized. Frances Hyland, when she assumed her military identity as Joan, wore black leotards and a short tunic with a sword belt. This was truly a bare-bones production but the complete immersion of the cast and the intensity with which it was performed made it come alive and remain in memory to a degree that no amount of costuming and scenery could have heightened. Much later Carl Hare devised Company One on a basis of simplicity and its offerings also were moving and memorable.

After Cothran left, the principal designer for the McPherson stage, working for both Bastion Theatre and Pacific Opera, was Jack Simon, a fine craftsman and an artist of lyrical vision. He was tragically removed from his promising career through a highway accident in the interior. At the Belfry Theatre there was Willie Heslup performing amazing illusionary feats of architecture on a stage that at the time lacked adequate depth to create perspective. When Bill West retired in 1985 Heslup became UVIC Theatre's designer, much to Bill's satisfaction. Later Heslup turned to the designing of movie sets which involved a move to the mainland, and Allan Stichbury became the Phoenix Theatre's designer.

Following the settling and re-establishment of the department, plans and architectural consultations began on a permanent theatre building on campus. Carl was involved in early stages until he left for Montreal to teach at the National Theatre School. As the building of the new Phoenix moved forward in the late seventies the faculty had complete input through every phase. According to Hare, one of the major reasons for this was the presence of West, since he was able to anticipate problems in the building as construction progressed.

One of the fortunate legacies from Dr. Allen's period was the decision by John Krich, the most gifted and versatile of the Victoria Fair group of actors, to remain at the university as a member of faculty. Krich has proven to be not only a fine actor and director, but also an inspiring teacher. Many of his students currently hold important posts in theatres across the country and may also be seen on films and television. Krich is also responsible for the development of the Phoenix Summer Theatre, a campus-based series which originated in 1972 and was not disbanded until 1993 when government support dried up.[1] The PST employed hundreds of students in "work study" situations for twenty years and provided Victoria with some memorable entertainment.

Once the theatre department was stabilized Barbara McIntyre retired from the chairmanship after having successfully completed a sensitive and difficult period of reconstruction. Finally, in the summer of 1981, after avoiding the commitment for many years, Carl

---

[1] The Department of Theatre reinstated the PST in the summer of 1994. (ed.)

Hare agreed to succeed her. A few months later, in November, it became his privilege to accept from the contractors the keys to the new state-of-the-art Phoenix Theatre.

This building, designed by Alan Lester, actually contains three theatres, two with 200 seats and the third, a flexible space, which seats about 60. The Roger Bishop Theatre, named after the originator of the theatre department, is a proscenium theatre with fly gallery for hoisting scenery, a small orchestra pit, capacious backstage space, and continental seating. The Dan George Theatre is named for British Columbia's notable late Native actor and has a thrust stage surrounded by the audience on three sides, with no member of the audience more than five rows from the actors. The McIntyre Studio is a smaller space with two levels of galleries permitting maximum flexibility in mounting different styles of staging and seating. Support areas include offices, a modern fully equipped scene shop, costume rooms with large storage spaces, and all facilities for designing and constructing costumes of every kind and period. Ancillary to all of this are studios and faculty and administrative offices. No students graduating from the theatre department can find themselves at a loss in the professional theatre when faced with the most advanced lighting and sound systems, as all theatres are fully equipped and flexible in these areas. The three lobbies flanking the theatre entrances flow into one another and may alternatively be used as rehearsal areas and even for *ad hoc* performances.

Attention to the importance of children's theatre is present in the studio theatre, where learning through children's games is demonstrated by means of a one-way mirror allowing students in Theatre-in-Education classes to observe children at play without the children becoming self-conscious. To quote Carl: "At the moment I seem to have come full circle. It's nice to have been involved in building two theatres. It's not an ego thing so much as a sense of completion. And now what we have is one of the finest education theatres in North America. It's not pretentious, just fully functional at a cost of $4.8 million, which is not one penny over the original budget we established in 1975."

When I reported in my Arts Dialogue column that the University of Victoria had signed a four-million-dollar contract for the building of a theatre complex on the Gordon Head campus, I was the recipient of numerous commentaries denouncing the outrageous and unjustifiable cost. The tenor of the remarks was to question the sanity of expending so much money on something that could not possibly be of financial value to the students in the long run. In the years since the well-designed, state-of-the-art theatre complex has been in service — literally the year round — graduating students have recorded many and notable success stories in television and film. Of equal importance is the quality of personal satisfaction and mental stimulation to be experienced in these types of careers. A life involved with the theatre, like any other occupation, is not a bed of roses the year round, but inevitably has its failures and disappointments. I have been told more than a few times by theatre people that "It's the only life that makes even the depressions worth struggling through. Once established in the theatrical life you take the lows with the highs, but you seldom seriously think of quitting."

A popular Vancouver actor once admitted to me that at any other job he might be earning at least three times what he was earning then, but would be without the heady challenges and the inner satisfaction he enjoys in the life he chose. Much the same story can be told by painters, sculptors, photographers, and musicians who are practising their art as a principal occupation. In a phrase, they could be richer but they could never be happier.

CHAPTER SIXTEEN

The Belfry Theatre

HERE are all the students who throng drama schools and university theatre departments going? What realistic goal can they expect to achieve? These teasers were posed at the start of a column written in October 1975. Many people had asked me this question. Their tone might be sceptical — or challenging. Either way their manner would imply that my answer, if I had one, would be vague and would not convince them no matter what my supportive evidence. A columnist lives a dangerous life, but I decided to tackle the subject anyway.

My response centred on a conversation I had had with Glynis Leyshon, who had recently married Richard Brownsey then finishing his Master's degree in public administration at UVIC. Glynis was on the threshold of a successful national career in theatre but this was not foreseeable at the time. She had been introduced to theatre at the age of 12 when she was chosen by her school principal in answer to a call from a North Vancouver theatre to play Helen Keller in their production of *The Miracle Worker.* This production, a solid success, was invited to stage a repeat performance at Vancouver's downtown Metro Theatre. "It was a fabulous experience," she recalled, but she felt she was not really committed to theatre at that time. Later she did two years of theatre at the University of British Columbia, but again the flame did not ignite.

"There were some excellent people there," she recalls, "but too few were really in love with the theatre. Instead, they were on ego trips, vying with each other, and full of the tensions occasioned by envy and anxiety." When she registered at UVIC it was to major in art history — "I was thinking of museum work. As an option in my

162

programme I decided to take one course in theatre and that was when I met Carl Hare. As a result of that I was one of the fortunate people since I had the opportunity to enter a professional situation right out of school. That opportunity was Carl's creation and was called Company One — it was quite unique. We had this tremendous creative thing, the chance to play before so many different audiences, to travel and be seen across the country."

When Glynis left the company in 1975 she had offers from many professional theatre groups across Canada. She chose to work as publicist with the Bastion Theatre which was going through a tremendous growth period. She dreamed, however, of being a producer with a small company of flexible actors.

Glynis's husband, Richard Brownsey, became manager of the renowned, but no longer extant, Anna Wyman Dance Company in Vancouver after completing his Master's at UVIC. At the same time Glynis enrolled in the Vancouver Playhouse theatre school where she studied for two years. Subsequently Brownsey was chosen to be administrator of the BC Cultural Services, thus bringing both gifted people back to Victoria.

It has been sixteen years since Glynis, poised on the threshold, talked to me about her dreams and her discoveries. In the meantime she has travelled through those years gathering experience, polishing technique in many areas, and always learning. Currently she is one of Canada's most gifted and experienced directors. But her anchor has remained in Victoria, where she is, in 1994, in her fifth season as artistic director of the flourishing Belfry Theatre. As well as planning Belfry seasons and frequently being called upon to direct across Canada, she is also engaged on occasion to stage productions for Pacific Opera Victoria as well as in Edmonton.

The Belfry Theatre is another of the remarkable success stories that have made bad prophets out of so many civic leaders over past several decades. The building was once occupied by a Baptist church whose congregation had moved to a new site. Since it was located in one of the city's older suburbs the site was not considered eminently desirable as a theatre except by those with strong aspirations and small means. Among its former users was by small dramatic company with the name, Springridge Theatre.[1]

The building's metamorphosis into a theatre began in 1976 and this seemed an appropriate use for a building that had served the public, both physically and spiritually, through several decades. The building was renovated — to a degree — and the plan put forward by a consortium of activists in the city's arts world was to rent it out for a wide spectrum of entertainment activities. Among those participating in an Open House festival on January 24, 1976, were the Victoria Conservatory of Music, Victoria Art Gallery, Bastion Theatre, Phoenix Theatre, Kaleidoscope Players, Theatre Guild, Victoria Symphony, Open Space, the Intercultural Society, Pacific Wind Quintet and Western Brass from the University of Victoria, the National Film Board, and Vancouver Playhouse.

With so broad and far-reaching an involvement it was obvious that an experienced hand, backed by intelligence, discernment, and imagination, was needed at the helm. A tall order. But Michael Stephen[2] and his associates who had sparked the concept were fortunate to find just such an individual in Don Shipley whose native city was propitiously Stratford, Ontario. Shipley had begun his career as a child actor in that city and rose to become assistant to Stratford Festival artistic director Robin Phillips. He had also run the Stratford theatre workshop for two years. He then spent some time travelling abroad before arriving on the west coast to become artistic director for Vancouver's Holiday Playhouse, a successful young people's theatre.

While he was there he "fell in love with what was being done at the Vancouver East Cultural Centre. So the decision was not difficult for me when I was invited, under a Local Initiatives Program (LIP) grant, to come to the Victoria neighbourhood centre. One important purpose of a cultural centre," he commented, "is to provide a

---

1 Springridge was the former name of the Fernwood district.
2 Son of Hugh Stephen, a former mayor of Victoria.

164

professionally equipped platform for performing arts events in such a moderately priced setting as this."

Don Shipley, Robert Montgomery, Gordon Reed, and Gina Purves-Hume were paid under the LIP grant to renovate, organize, and direct the centre's operation. The grant did not encompass materials, "So we are having to cadge from all sorts of sources," Don told me as we toured the area which was to become a performance space. Rows of old but reasonably comfortable seats, which were on loan from an Esquimalt warehouse, were waiting to be spruced up and installed. A valued acquisition was an old-style but blessedly noiseless fan that was suspended from the ceiling. "It will move the warm air about instead of allowing it to settle in a hot canopy over the balcony while people on the ground floor shiver," Shipley explained.

"At present there is no money for me to originate any productions at the Belfry but everything can't be done at once. We have applied for a BC Cultural Fund grant and are pinning our faith on that." Later the grant came through and the theatre project was on its way.

The name chosen for the new/old performance space with its steepled bell tower was inevitable, "The Belfry." To me it seemed a singularly appropriate title. Thereafter I had to avoid the temptation in my reviews, to use the pejorative "bats" (or even "ding-a-lings") in the belfry, or even to describe some performance as "a resounding success."

At first the Belfry played host to a miscellany of musical and other presentations, mostly local, but some originating from mainland centres. Then came its first self-generated product and it was a winner. With a provincial cultural grant in hand Don Shipley, together with gifted mainlander Pat Armstrong, created a revue based on the music of Irving Berlin titled *Puttin' on the Ritz*. The cast consisted of a quartet of talented and popular Victoria entertainers including Mary Swinton, Dan Costain, Sheila McCarthy, and Bill Hosie. The mood and period were highlighted by a black-and-white art deco set designed by Ken MacDonald, a versatile wardrobe in the same monochromatic scheme accented to the right degree by some silver glitter, with the whole beautifully lit by Giles Hogya.[3]

The musical arrangement for *Puttin' on the Ritz* was in itself quite special, avoiding sentimentality but remaining sensitive to the moods of Berlin's songs and their engaging rhythms. The collaboration reunited Vancouver musician Joan Beckow and Shipley in a partnership that had originated in Vancouver where both were involved with the city's Holiday Playhouse. Joan had written lyrics and music for four university shows during her attendance at UCLA. Two of them had been homecoming shows in which a vivacious co-student named Carol Burnett played the lead.

Puttin' on the Ritz was successful beyond anyone's most optimistic forecast. It ran for several extended weeks and then was invited to play during the summer in the (now sadly vanished) David Y. H. Lui Theatre in Vancouver, where it became known as the best seasonal entertainment in town. It was also destined for a long run at Stratford until difficulties involving rights forced it to close after only a few performances.

There are probably few undertakings more knife-edged than mounting an original production on a modest budget and then waiting for business to heat up at the box office. When this happens, however, there is nothing more positive for encouraging entrepreneurs to go forward to the next enterprise. At the Belfry Shipley stirred a spicy brew by mixing some of the best local talents with Canadian imports who had made names for themselves elsewhere. Included among these were a memory-haunting production of Canadian playwright Joanna Glass's *Canadian Gothic*, the Toronto-based Theatre Passe Muraille's excellent and highly original *Farm Show*, and some memorable jazz concerts. The savour of this shakedown cruise, for those of us who took it all in, has lasted through the years.

---

3   Hogya is currently lighting designer and professor in the University of Victoria theater department, interspersing his duties with intervals of lighting stages and directing in New York's off-Broadway theatres.

Intense audience-approval was also chalked up by more than one self-generated production. Among these was the musical biography of the legendary Paris street singer Edith Piaf, a heart-rending Cinderella story *sans* happy ending that was mounted in 1978. Co-directors Shipley and Pat Armstrong achieved a sensitively coherent melding of the essential parts of Piaf's life — the rise and fall, the restoration to international stardom, and then the early death. It was a poignant portrayal of the loving, vital person who had evolved from the street waif, known affectionately by Parisians, as "the little sparrow."

Guest artist Pauline LeBel profoundly evoked Piaf's character and charm, her irresistible appeal and poignancy with an emotion that was sincere and a voice that was well able to convey her emotions. Shipley's sense of the aesthetic and finely tuned dramatic perception were reflected in the simplicity of the production and the understatement of the set design and lighting respectively by Ken MacDonald and Giles Hogya. The music director was again Joan Beckow who arranged the excellent score. The musicians were lead by Victoria pianist Chris Donison who has continued to be one of the city's busiest professional artists, particularly in the difficult and very special field of accompaniment and ensemble performance.

Piaf opened on 27 October with sellouts during the originally scheduled run, as well as standing ovations. Performances were extended for a total run of three weeks. Ironically that final performance came on the day my weekly column dealt with the latest government assault singling out the arts for budget cuts. The eight-column head stated "Arts Budget Cuts Force Belfry to Fight for its Life."

Co-incidentally I had that week interviewed one of Canada's leaders in the arts field at the time, Canadian National Ballet director Celia Franca. She pulled no punches: "Canada's artists," she stated, "have definitely subsidized the arts throughout the cultural history of Canada." Continuing, she pointed out that "because they are among the most convinced and dedicated of people — probably only equalled in their zeal by pure scientists — they are mostly inadequately paid and have to get along without the fringe benefits the rest of us take for granted. Artists are singular in that they do not operate on the 'so many dollars so many hours principle.' They are in fact about all that is left in our society of the old-world craftsman to whom the perfection of his product was paramount. There is still no such thing as nine-to-five hours for an artist in the midst of creating or practising within his craft."

While musicians' unions and CAEA prescribe the number of hours a performer may work within a certain pay scale — that is, rehearse or appear publicly — don't imagine that the dedicated artist's work is over at the end of a scheduled rehearsal. Actors study scripts, memorize lines, and seek more clues to characterization and in-depth analysis of scenes. Dancers work unceasingly on their bodies which are their instruments, and musicians spend hundreds of hours in studio practise and thinking through the score. Any business-man or woman who can claim an equal or greater involvement is probably also being paid in at least the neighbourhood of $75,000 annually. All of this makes it doubly unfair that governments, when they decide to launch an economic blitz, choose the arts as their principal target.

The Belfry had made its annual application to Canada Council for $10,000, hoping to receive $7,000. They were turned down completely. A bid for $25,000 from the BC Cultural Fund netted $15,000, an increase over the previous year but one that came nowhere near the rate of inflation nor offset the lack of federal support. Shipley commented: "We are aware that we are not alone in the matter. Our colleagues all across the country are similarly affected and we are grateful for the assistance we are getting from BC. The fact is not altered that the Belfry's future looks very dark at this moment. Of course we are going to try to do something for ourselves and we expect to come up with fund-raising plans very soon."

With a vigorously pursued self-help programme and consider-able community support the Belfry survived that crisis. The theatre was rented by a variety of groups and artists including the once-active Victoria Youth Theatre. Other activities included family film showings, concerts, and dance events. The public responded to the Belfry's self-help campaign and the dreaded closing of its doors did not happen.

Following Don Shipley's decision to leave the city in 1980, a new director was sought and the choice made was an easterner, James Roy. Young and already successful, Roy's interest in theatre was born when, as a grade nine student, he saw his first live play. It was Tennessee Williams' *The Glass Menagerie.* The experience turned him into an overnight theatre buff. Participation in high school productions led him to studies in theatre, including design and direction, at York University. He spent a season in Britain working with the Duke's Playhouse Company in Lancaster, an experience that broadened his perspective.

After returning to Toronto he worked with the city's Theatre Passe Muraille before starting his own theatre in the tiny town of Blyth, Ontario in 1975. At that time it had a population of 900. Surprisingly, there was also a theatre that would seat a little over half that number. There were, of course, those people who considered it a foolish venture, but the festival grew and in 1979, 20,000 people saw the plays in an expanded and improved theatre.

James Roy came to the Belfry undisturbed by Ontarians telling him "there's not much to do in Victoria." "On the contrary," he commented during an interview, "with two professional theatres and several non-professional companies, the university, Camosun College, the symphony, festivals, opera, dance — it's a busy scene." Roy came to the Belfry with a defined policy based on what had already been established and on his own experience: a blend of moods, a season to include some emphasis on Canadian works, one Broadway highlight, and a musical revue.

The highlight of his first season however, turned out to be none of the above, and one of the Belfry's most memorable experiences was Roy's production of *On Golden Pond.* The show starred Frances Hyland and Donald Davis, both Canadian actors with international reputations on stage, in film, and on television. Carl Hare, Karen Austin, and Andrew Sabiston completed the cast.

Roy was not long at the Belfry and the 1984-85 season came under the rule of Miles Potter, a Toronto-based actor and director with experience in television and radio. Potter's first season opened with two Canadian premières: the London hit, *Quartermaine's Terms*, billed as a comedy but with deeper veins of poignancy and unresolved problems, and Marsha Norman's 1938 Pulitzer Prize winner *Night Mother*, a deeply sensitive drama but difficult to produce. Potter left Victoria at the end of the 1985-86 season.

In 1977 Don Shipley had directed Joanna M. Glass's pair of short plays — *Canadian Gothic* and *American Modern*, which included Glynis Leyshon in her first Belfry appearance. Glynis had by then already toured Canada for two years with Carl Hare's Company One and directed in Toronto as well as for Bastion Theatre. In Potter's last year with the Belfry, Leyshon had guest-directed the season-ender, Willy Russell's entertaining two-character charmer, *Educating Rita*. This proved to be one of the Belfry's most unforgettable successes. No one was to know at that time that Leyshon would become the latest in a long line of Belfry artistic directors.

With the acquisition of the entire building in 1991 when the hostel Cool Aid (which had occupied a part of the complex) moved, the Belfry launched a carefully planned expansion that did not centre on a greatly enlarged audience accommodation for the main stage. The rationale was that the intimate style of theatre that had functioned so successfully for eighteen years had many advantages. There is a close communion between an audience whose furthest distance from the stage is no more than sixty feet.

The main benefit of these renovations includes a greatly increased backstage area allowing appropriate crossover space for actors and stage crew, as well as less restricted set design parameters, a well-deserved plus for the several gifted stage designers who have over the years achieved astonishing effects under difficult circumstances. Additionally, there is now a well-equipped workshop for the design and building of sets, a costume studio, and a properties storage area. Roomier dressing rooms and related conveniences are also in place.

Front-of-house alterations have provided a new entrance into a spacious lobby area, now including a coffee bar. Most exciting for the director and personnel has been the addition of a studio theatre where twenty-first-century exploratory theatre as well as productions for young audiences can be presented. This space also provides promising new playwrights with the experience of having their scripts workshopped. When not otherwise occupied the studio theatre is available for renting for various kinds of presentations, including dance recitals and musical events.

The Belfry is small enough to be intimate and, because it has not been forced into primarily box office-influenced choices, it has brought to the city many notable experiences that otherwise might have been unavailable. It has offered us works by some of the most perceptive and colourful writers of our time, including Hugh Leonard's delightful and haunting Tony Award winner *Da*, and A. R. Gurney's *The Dining Room* and *Children*, the latter a Rockefeller Playwriting Award winner. British playwright Peter Nichols' poignant *A Day in the Life of Joe Egg* and David Pownall's compelling portrait of tyranny in action, *Master Class*, have also been significant productions. In addition, Canadian playwrights of talent have consistently found a showcase on the small but effective stage.

While once considered too "out of the way" to be viable, the Belfry's steady growth stands out in relation to all other attempts to established professional theatre in the city. Unquestionably, its few failures were due to such factors as rents being far out of proportion to the maximum potential at the box office. The Belfy is one of Victoria's important assets and continues to be directed with professional skill, imagination, and taste by Glynis Leyshon as it nears its twentieth birthday.

Bastion and the Belfry, however, were not the only professional theatres to develop in Victoria, and an important part was played by Kaleidoscope in more recent years.

❦

CHAPTER SEVENTEEN

Kaleidoscope Theatre

W HILE the Belfry was getting on with the additions and alterations to its recently acquired premises, a new specifically designed, company-owned theatre building was added to the Victoria arts scene by the now long-established Kaleidoscope Theatre, with only Langham Court, the Victoria Theatre Guild's home for almost six decades, being debt free. Retaining amateur status and therefore avoiding Equity costs, the Guild could use the city's many gifted amateur actors and backstage workers to produce regular seasons of former Broadway and London successes, their principal out-of-town costs being royalties.

When it appeared to Canada Council that there needed to be some strengthening of the Bastion Theatre before making major grants, not only did it provide funds for Edwin Stephenson to direct a main stage production but in December 1970 provided a grant to bring Colin Gorrie to Victoria to direct Tennessee Williams' *Summer and Smoke.* In the late summer of that year Gorrie, a graduate architect who worked in film and television, returned to assist Mrs. Simpson-Baikie in management and to direct Bastion school and workshop productions.

Gorrie's wife, Elizabeth, rich in theatre experience stretching from Brantford, Ontario, to the west coast was also came on a Canada Council grant to work with the Bastion Theatre School. Also teaching in the School as well as directing the touring company was Paul Liittich. This trio of imaginative theatre people were to become major assets to the city's arts scene.

Paul's acting career had begun in Brantford, Ontario, and it became his profession in 1969 while with Brantford's Total Theatre under the direction of Elizabeth Gorrie. In 1970 he came to the west coast and in 1971 joined the Bastion Theatre Company. He continued to exercise his talents in mime and the language of movement in many Kaleidoscope productions. His range was impressive, from Bastion's company shows to Kaleidoscope's production of *Cabaret* and Jerry Gosley's summer *Smile Show*.

Kaleidoscope Theatre was created by Paul Liittich, Jim Netherton, and Barbara MacLaughlin with an LIP grant, the primary intention being to work for and with physically handicapped and emotionally disturbed children. Regular schools were also visited, this being a form of self-therapy. Liittich commented, "It is necessary to the quality of our performance that we receive from time to time, normal reactions to what we are doing ... a kind of mirror we can test ourselves by."

Some highly imaginative and original action on the schools circuit was seen under the grant. The following year it was the only LIP project in Greater Victoria to be funded a second time. Inevitably there is a relationship between existence at or below the poverty line and a youngster's emotional problems. This aspect was approached by Kaleidoscope early in 1975 with ten weeks of free theatre workshops. The response was an enrolment of one hundred and ten youngsters ranging in age from five to sixteen years.

On flying visits to Victoria during Kaleidoscope's first year, Elizabeth Gorrie worked with the ensemble that included Dan Costain, Barbara Poggemiller, Carole Boer, and Karen Kramer. All were either theatre school graduates, dancers, or musicians. To avoid encroaching on Bastion Theatre's School it was agreed that youngsters seeking to enrol in Kaleidoscope workshops come from families unable to meet Bastion's moderate tuition fees.

In its first year, Kaleidoscope created *The Magic Stone* for grades 1 to 3, a pirate show for grades 4 to 7, and pre-school shows based on story theatre technique and including a puppet show. It also prepared Liz Gorrie's adaptation of *The Musicians of Bremen*.

A high standard of acting is of first importance in children's theatre. This is not to say that young audiences are unaffected by the story being told, but if the actors telling it are not on their toes, playing with conviction and imagination, attention can wander and the youngsters generally will be unimpressed. It is essential that the acting be competent, vital, and rich in imagination.

Children make an intent and critical audience. They are as quick to detect sloppiness and insincerity as they are to respond in a positive way to invention. Scenery and props can be minimal because a child's imagination takes over in that department. Costumes can be sketchy but must be colourful. For teachers, school boards, and parents it is important to recognize that children's theatre can instruct much more indelibly and at an earlier age than most other ways of imparting facts and ideas. In schools that have been visited by Kaleidoscope, teachers report that discussions continue for days and often weeks following the performance.

While Kaleidoscope concentrated on children's theatre, the company occasionally produced shows aimed at adult audiences. For those who saw Kaleidoscope's production of *Cabaret* in which Liittich played the role of the emcee made famous by Joel Gray in the movie version, the memory remains indelible. This production was something of a revelation of what artistry in lighting and mood-creation could do for an ordinary platform stage in a gymnasium more accustomed to basketball, and banquets. In proper cabaret style the audience was seated at small tables and drawn into the action by the peripatetic lure of the Berlin Kit Kat Club emcee who prowled among them with the sleekness and magnetism of a graceful jungle cat. Director Colin Gorrie understood the tempo and the sense of tension in a Berlin poised on the brink of war and this, together with Jack Simon's uncluttered, highly functional set and Giles Hogya's imaginative lighting design made this 1976 Kaleidoscope adult presentation one to linger long in memory. Vancouver actress Pat Armstrong, seen on other occasions at the Belfry, and Jean-Paul Destrubé were effective in poignant roles.

By the end of 1975 Elizabeth Gorrie was installed as full-time director of the company. It was then that Kaleidoscope began its expansion to reach, through schools and other institutions, the minds and sensitivities of as many children as possible. An important aspect of Kaleidoscope's work is that all the material is original. The only scripts used are those that evolve through the company's own improvisations and are then honed and polished into their most effective form. Wildly joyful fantasies are conjured up at work sessions and many of them become, in a way, classical. One such piece had the rhythmic chanting title — *Alihiparhinocrocadillagator!* — tongue-twister and a fast-paced energetic romp that young audiences adored.

Over the next four years Kaleidoscope developed rapidly, becoming acknowledged Canada-wide as an exemplary educational tool to enhance creativity and knowledge at all stages of growth. Among its achievements was the development of three museum extension theatre programs in combination with the Royal British Columbia Museum. These culminated in a nationally sponsored tour with the Manitoba Museum of Man and Nature. The company was also commissioned by the Secretary of State to write, produce, and tour *Mon Pays/My Country* — a play about Canada from the point of view of a French-Canadian *habitant*.

In 1977 Paul Gallico's poignant story *The Snow Goose* was developed by Elizabeth Gorrie into a play for Kaleidoscope. It was performed by the company in Toronto at the Canadian and Youth Drama Association conference which coincided with the annual meeting of the Association Internationale du Théâtre pour les Enfants et la Jeunesse. It was described by experts as "the best thing that has come into the schools," and a performance of it at the University of Ottawa was followed by an invitation to perform at the National Arts Centre "at the earliest possible moment." The invitation included prepaid return air transportation.

At this conference Kaleidoscope conducted a mask construction workshop and attended some other children's theatre group performances, including six French companies from Quebec and Sudbury and the Paper Bag Company from New York. Elizabeth noted how critical the audiences were and something less than generous in applause. When it was time for Kaleidoscope to present *The Snow Goose* before an audience that included Russian, Cuban,

Israeli, Czech, Yugoslavian, Rumanian, French, and German representatives, Elizabeth admits she was nervous.

"Standing in the wings during the performance, I couldn't tell what the reaction was" she commented. "Then suddenly at the end they were all standing, clapping, and cheering." David Peacock, Canada Council head of theatre at the time, described the performance as "a beautiful experience." Following this the word around Toronto and Ottawa was that Canada's best in children's theatre was to be found in Victoria. As a spin-off from this performance Gorrie was invited by the Israeli government to direct a production of *The Snow Goose* for Israel's National Theatre for Children and Youth in 1978.

Several months later Kaleidoscope conceived and hosted Canada's first International Theatre Festival for Young People as a part of a Heritage Festival in Vancouver. In 1978 Kaleidoscope was commissioned by the BC Government's Bicentennial Celebrations Committee to produce a summer travelling musical based on the life of Captain Cook. They were also commissioned in 1979 by the Canadian Book Week committee to produce a family show based on Canadian books to mark the International Year of the Child, and by the Manitoba Museum of Man and Nature to create a docudrama about European settlement in Western Canada. This was to tour as part of a National Museum exhibition. In the same year the company was selected to go to Britain as Canada's representative to the International Eisteddfod in Wales.

In 1980 they were selected to perform at the 1981 American National Showcase of Performing Arts for Young People (Birmingham, Alabama), were chosen by Canada Council to represent Canada at the Theatre in Education conference in London, England, among other honours. At home, some excellent work was done in conjunction with the Victoria Symphony Orchestra when the company created and performed visual interpretations of the music with the orchestra. This was highly popular with the primary grade children and it continued for five seasons.

Kaleidoscope was later invited to bring its company to Tokyo to perform in the National Children's Castle and as a result of a successful visit, Japan's renowned creator of children's theatre Yukio Sekiya accepted an invitation to visit Victoria and develop a play with Kaleidoscope students. This was a complete success.

The episode led me into the rare experience of interviewing an artist in a completely unknown language. French I could have handled with some assurance, in Spanish or Italian I might have made progress, and in German, providing we were discussing music, the passage would have been bumpy but not altogether unintelligible. So my questions were directed to Sekiya through an interpreter with the answers returning to me in English. To feel one is inadequate on such an occasion is ridiculous, but nevertheless I did so feel during the interview. But I had prepared myself with what could at least pass for an apology. Maurice, who learned to speak and read Japanese during the Second World War, provided me with an appropriate phrase for conclusion of the interview: "Domo arigato gozi mas."[1] Yukio Sekiya responded with smiles and deep bows and I was told afterward that he considered that I had done him great honour.

Kaleidoscope finally gained its own home for rehearsal and public performance when it purchased an old building on Herald Street in 1991. With the help of public and private funding they renovated and designed the interior in tune with their small-theatre requirements. Perhaps no one in the theatre community deserves more recognition for his devotion and unswerving loyalty to the theatre community than the late Hugh Henderson. His years of devotion to both Kaleidoscope and the Bastion through unfailing financial generosity and significant moral support will not soon be forgotten. It is apt that his name should grace the new Kaleidoscope theatre.

Not long after the Kaleidoscope Theatre started under Liittich, and attracted the participation of the Gorries, it became apparent that the new enterprise was beckoning to those young men and women who were dedicated products of the University of Victoria theatre school. Among them was Jim Leard, a graduate of the

---

[1] The polite form of "thank you." (ed.)

Theatre Department, and an imaginative script arranger and play maker who was mainly responsible for creating what is now known far and wide as Story Theatre. This project had been welcomed and enthusiastically received all over the continent, including such prestigious places as the Smithsonian Institute and Wolf Trap. Its audience concentration ranges from kindergarten to grade six. Within this range Leard uses the schools' reading programmes in preparing scripts, thus animating and intensifying the language arts for those age groups experiencing an early introduction.

Its ventures into different cultures, legends, lifestyles and folklore has greatly enriched Kaleidoscope and Story Theatre. Being much more than mere imitators, the two companies have created new growth, weaving the varied influences, beliefs, social patterns and legends into what is native to its own natural environment. What has emerged is a composite theatre that is exceedingly rich in its power to integrate the ancient past with the vital present and to construct creatively on such a foundation, theatre works that are fresh and evocative and send audiences of every age on their way, not soon to forget the experience.

Not to be forgotten in the arts annals of this part of the world are the contributions made by the many visual artists who came to know and love the West Coast so well. The story of the visual arts in Victoria is essentially the story of the origins and development of the Art Gallery of Greater Victoria which, among other accomplishments, has served to display our visual history so well.

CHAPTER EIGHTEEN

The Art Gallery of Greater Victoria

EFORE the Hudson's Bay Company's trading post expanded to become the City of Victoria, among those who settled here there were artists of vision and imagination in many media. Prominent among these were individuals skilled in the relatively new medium of photography as well as those competent with pencil, charcoal, and watercolour. As for local native art, the weavings and carvings of the Coast Salish were, for most newcomers, incomprehensible and hardly worthy of the term art. How things were to change with respect to the latter in the decades to come.

It was inevitable that creative people — those with vision and imagination who delighted in the fall of light on a rock face, the sifting of sunlight among tall trees, and the changing moods of sea and lake — should find on Vancouver's Island a land of endless inspiration. Time has proved that the most vivid talent to soar within the first quarter of the twentieth century was that of Emily, youngest daughter of Richard Carr, Esq. Recognized in her lifetime by only a few Victorians as an artist of great vision, her many paintings and sketches were more often ridiculed than admired. Around Victoria she was generally regarded as quite eccentric and "different."

In her last years of declining health, however, she captured the attention and admiration of important people on the mainland and in the east. This occurred largely through the friendship and enthusiasm of a few high-profile persons such as the American artist Mark Tobey, the Group of Seven's Lawren Harris, and W. H. Clarke of the Toronto publishing firm Clarke-Irwin. Among her champions were Flora Hamilton Burns and Willie Newcombe in Victoria, and Ira Dilworth of the CBC. She had at least two highly successful showings of her work at the Vancouver Art Gallery and in major art circles across Canada Emily Carr's name began cropping up with increasing frequency. She was not to have a proper showing of her work in Victoria, however, until long after her death.

Emily died in 1945, naming Ira Dilworth as her literary executor and Lawren Harris to dispose of her art. She left many paintings and sketches stacked up in her Victoria studio which would later become priceless. Unfortunately, Carr's home town had little to offer at the time of her death in the way of an appropriate home for her many works — not that many recognized their significance. There was no such thing as a climate-controlled, secure, and spacious gallery in the capital city nor, it seemed, likely ever to be.

Carr was not the only gifted and knowledgeable artist in Victoria, though certainly the most innovative. The city included, in fact, many artists who were original, technically competent, distinctive in style, and masters of more than one medium. There was Sophie Pemberton (later Deane-Drummond), Emily's girlhood acquaintance, whose specialty was portraiture and the human figure. Ina Uhthoff, a technically versatile and unique artist and teacher, was also living in Victoria in Emily's later years.

Ina had come to Victoria from the Interior with her two young children in 1926. In her native Scotland she had received a thorough training at the Glasgow School of Art under the famous Charles Rennie Mackintosh. Apart from this background she arrived in Victoria with a full share of Scots integrity and courage and not much else.

Immediately, she established a teaching studio which eventually became so well regarded that the provincial Department of Education asked her to take over its Kingston Street Pottery School and turn it into a general school of art. There she taught painting, drawing, commercial art, linocut printing, clay sculpture, and pottery. She was also the school janitor, arriving at seven in the morning on winter days to light the furnace and clean the classrooms. This school thrived until financial constraints during the Second World War compelled the government to close it, whereupon Ina returned to private teaching and also added her very considerable skill to a movement which would result in the creation of the Art Gallery of Greater Victoria.

It is not too much to say that Ina Uhthoff sacrificed much of her career as a painter in order unstintingly to serve the gallery's interests. It was lucky for the institution that, in spite of a very traditional training, she was open minded toward all new forms of art and, indeed, towards the end of her career was painting abstractions herself. She died in 1971 at the age of 82.

Other artists who would later put Victoria on the map included Jack Shadbolt, whose current continent-wide reputation had its origin in his native Victoria; Will Menelaws, an exceptional commercial artist and teacher; and now internationally noted portrait artist Myfanwy Pavelic, a niece of Sara Spencer who was to make possible Victoria's first and only public art gallery. Later came Carole Sabiston, a profoundly original fabric artist who is recognized across Canada. Her work is seen in panels and banners, on the walls of major public buildings, in altar cloths, and in the theatre. Further international success is present in the award-winning prints of Pat Martin Bates and the vivid paintings of Michael Morris and Herbert Siebner.

When one surveys the city's fine arts scene, recognizes its calibre, and notices the extent of its attainment since the turn of the century, it is all the more astonishing that until the fall of 1952 gallery walls for properly lit showings of artists' work were virtually non-existent in the city. When I first began a general coverage of the arts for the *Times* before the Second World War I saw shows in the ante-room of the former dining room at the Hudson's Bay' store, in the Georgian Lounge and private dining rooms of the Empress Hotel, at the YM-YWCA, and in a variety of other equally pleasant but, technically speaking, unsatisfactory venues. In an earlier period agricultural fairs were one of the few places providing limited space to local artists such as Sophie Pemberton, who was given a one-woman show at the fair of 1901.

In the 1920s a few arts-knowledgeable people assembled a series of loans from local collections for display at the new Crystal

Gardens. There was also the Island Arts and Crafts Society (which had been formed in 1909) that held annual displays of its members' work. These were, however, episodic events that gave no permanent nor complete survey of the general and versatile enterprise of residents of the lower island. Even at these limited showings the exploration of new techniques and concepts by new-wave artists such as Carr, Shadbolt, Max Maynard, and Edythe Hembroff were largely ignored. In 1932 Island Arts and Crafts begrudgingly provided a "modern" room in its annual show. This was a first and a last for Island Arts and Crafts, for three of the four artists represented left shortly thereafter to explore a broader field in the more stimulating atmosphere of Vancouver.

In Victoria at that time most art-conscious people paid tribute to the atmospheric charm of elegant watercolours by Miss Josephine Crease. She lived out her life on the family estate "Pentrelew" on Fort Street where the Victoria Truth Centre now stands. There appeared no stimulus capable of challenging public indifference to the arts, including the long-rooted anti-arts attitude of city councils and therefore (it was presumed) of the public at large. However, quietly but determinedly, winds of change were stirring and would soon make themselves felt.

As the city moved on into the mid-thirties little changed in Victoria's arts world with the exception of a continued growth in the area of music study and performance. As for the pictorial arts they appeared, if any movement at all was discernible, to be keeping time to a turn-of-the-century tune, with one notable exception. The most vital and exhilarating activity was taking place at this time in the studio of Ina Uhthoff, where she taught and inspired a large number of students in numerous techniques and all media. I was at her school for almost a year, having finally reached out toward my earliest joy, my first dream. I relished every moment of this experience but it all ended when my father became ill with terminal cancer and I left art school to help nurse him.

After my father died we sold the four-bedroom home on its acre of manicured garden and moved to a smaller, single-level house in Oak Bay. It was on two good-sized-lots dotted with nine mature oak trees and a mini-orchard and gave us plenty of the privacy that my mother craved. Having said a regretful goodbye to further art school training I was soon back, reluctantly, to teaching music and the prospect of doing some more writing. My old typewriter came out of covers and was established in my bedroom. From it came some poetry, articles, and stories — even a play.

Thoughts of the art school and all that I had learned within a few months remained alive, especially the satisfaction I had found in the process of the hand printing medium using lino or wood blocks. As for my small grand piano, it remained closed and draped most of the time — except when mother sighed over it and recalled the hundreds of hours I'd spent with the classics — Beethoven, Schumann, Bach, Chopin, Ravel, and Debussy. To please her I played off and on in the mornings, taught a few youngsters in the afternoons, and in the evenings I wrote, or sketched ideas for wood or lino blockprints.

After moving to Oak Bay I soon discovered an incredible bonus. The daughter of a former owner of the house we were living in had, it seemed, been an artist who specialized in several print techniques. A small studio adjoined the rear garden, and when I had time to explore it I discovered — of all wonderful prizes — a hand printing press. The studio had a large north-facing window and small high windows on the west side where it abutted onto the garage roof. Often at night, when I was working on my lino cuts, there would be a light scratching sound and I would look up to see an audience of two or three raccoons, their masked faces gazing in on me and my work.

Queries of the owner's agents elicited the information that the young artist had gone to Europe and we were free to use the roller press if we wished. Of course I did use it and in our first three Christmases in the house I was able to print all our own cards and even take personal orders from several of my mother's friends. I also managed to retain my contact with Ina Uhthoff, and this association was to place me at centre stage when the first moves were made towards the concept of establishing an art gallery in the city.

It was inevitable that a city superbly garnished by nature, amiable in climate, and unflurried in pace — isolated, as medieval castles were protected by their surrounding moats — should attract many people of wealth. Large homes were soon established and some were filled with valuable art objects, including important collections from various exotic areas of the world. When there were no family members of discernment waiting in the wings, such collections were often dispersed, either intact through brokers or, more regrettably, in lots through auction. In this manner many important local collections became lost to the community since there was no local repository to which they could be donated.

A case in point is the story of John and Catherine Maltwood, who retired to Victoria in the early 1930s bringing with them a superb collection of artifacts from many countries. They purchased an acreage on West Saanich Road and bought an appealing and spacious residence of Tudor design to house themselves and their exotic collection. When health concerns became crucial the Maltwoods made the decision to leave the residence and property to the Municipality of Saanich and their rare, virtually priceless, collection to the City of Victoria together with sufficient funds to build a gallery to house it.

John Maltwood made the offer in a letter addressed to the mayor and council. When he received no reply he wrote again requesting a meeting with the council to lay his plans before them. Finally, and with an obvious lack of enthusiasm, a day and time were established, but when he went to the meeting only two aldermen turned up. Disgusted, Maltwood withdrew his offer, vowing that the city would never have his collection. Well-known Victoria artist and teacher John Kyle had accompanied Maltwood to the "meeting." Kyle expressed the opinion that the council saw no need for a public gallery in Victoria and were determined not to be stuck with the upkeep of such a facility. What they would have known, had they done Maltwood the simple courtesy of listening to his proposition, was that he was prepared to partially endow the necessary building.

184

Maltwood's next effort was to offer his collection to the provincial government. Sixteen months passed as the government gave the proposition its "deep-six" treatment. Maltwood's patience had come to an end. He transferred the offer to the University of British Columbia as a future bequest, together with sufficient endowment funds to make it worthwhile for UBC to accept. However, Victoria was to inherit it after all. When news of Victoria College's expansion into university status was announced, John Maltwood immediately transferred his bequest intact to the new University of Victoria. Subsequently, the Maltwood legacy became part of the University's already extensive collection and the Maltwood Gallery, located in the University Centre complex, has become a focus and a landmark facility on the campus.

The winds of war in Europe, however, brought us one remarkable piece of good fortune — the presence in our city of the Honourable Mark Kearley. This gifted son of Viscount Portsmouth had come with his wife and three children to settle in Metchosin for the duration. Accustomed to finding respectable state or civic galleries wherever he went in Europe or Britain, Kearley was astounded to find so beautiful a city — the capital, moreover, of a huge province — lacking even a modest version of a civic art gallery. He quickly discovered that the city was home to a number of distinctly talented and interesting artists, especially Emily Carr, to whose work he had soon been introduced.

An instinctive mover and innovator not accustomed to leaving his ideas and thoughts on other people's doorsteps for possible action, Kearley soon brought together an informal committee to discuss what could be done about the situation. At the first meeting of the group a first step was taken with the agreement to form a Victoria branch of the Federation of Canadian Artists. It was further decided to immediately set about the procuring of rental premises for use as a temporary gallery.

At that time, the Federation of Canadian Artists was a nation-wide body and was the only Canadian agency which continuously circulated travelling exhibitions. The new Victoria branch quickly achieved sufficient muscle to induce about forty members to sign up, of which I was one. Chaired by Kearley, the first executive board consisted of Ina Uhthoff, Isabel Hobbs, Will Menelaws, G. H. Parker, and C. J. Turgeon. The headmistress of St. Margaret's School, Miss Mary Pearce, hearing of the movement, offered the use of the school auditorium for lectures and meetings.

The first exhibition sponsored by the branch took place at the Empress Hotel and consisted of the work of Chang Shu-Qi. In the meantime the membership had grown to seventy. The following February the branch arranged a showing of paintings and sketches by members of the armed forces at Prince Robert House, a local military hostel. A week later Lawren Harris came from Vancouver to give a talk on the Group of Seven.

The Kearley group continued to sponsor exhibitions, lectures, and film showings whenever they could and Kearley was soon able to report that the Victoria group constituted both numerically and financially the strongest branch within the FCA. Income from lectures and shows totalled $1,500.

The search for a gallery showroom went on and finally ended successfully, if temporarily, when Thomas Plimley's automobile display room at 965 Yates Street (on the southwest corner of Yates and Quadra Streets) became available. The car industry had not yet fully converted from wartime production, which meant that private automobiles were still in short supply.

In order to keep in the public mind the fact that the premises were merely a holding operation, pending the acquisition of a proper and permanent civic gallery, Kearley decided on the modest title, "The Little Centre." As such it was formally opened on 19 July 1946 by Governor-General Viscount Alexander.

In the course of its first year the Little Centre was host to fifteen exhibitions, which included works by Lawren Harris, the Canadian Group of Painters, and the Ontario Society of Artists. Local artists were also represented, including Sophie Deane-Drummond, Ronald Bladen (who was to become an outstanding sculptor in the United States), Stella Langdale, and W. J. B. Newcombe. In addition, seventeen lectures with films were presented, including the première of the National Film Board's profile of Emily Carr, *Klee Wyck*.

Thanks to all those who gave of their time and energy freely, and more specifically to originator Mark Kearley's European experience as well as Ina Uhthoff's open-minded acceptance of what was vital and imaginative, the Little Centre was bringing fresh cultural breezes into the city. This included, for example, the city's first introduction to reproductions of the widely heralded works of the French impressionists and post-impressionists.

At the end of that year the society decided that the FCA's latest demands for a minimum 40% of local member's fees was too much to sustain and therefore withdrew from that association. Kearley announced his resignation at the same time, as he and his family were returning to Switzerland. His successor in the chair was B. R. Berrick, a retired English businessman who had found time to cultivate a talent for watercolour to the point where he was producing work of professional calibre.

In the early days of the gallery movement many individuals became highly effective promoters of the visual arts. These included Major Cuthbert Holmes, who joined the board in 1946, and Sara Spencer, the arts-loving and decisive daughter of business magnate David Spencer, Sr. She was a woman who knew her own mind and was never about to be cowed by a group of parochially minded city councillors. Other prime movers included painters Gladys Ewan and Molly Privett, chief public librarian Margaret Clay, and Mrs. Pamela Austin, who, with her husband, Tom, was later to become curator of the UVIC's Maltwood Art Gallery. Another vital contributor was Gwen Scott. Until her retirement a few years before her death in 1981 Scott had run a long-established and charming book store on Douglas Street. At her death it was discovered that she had bequeathed much of her fairly substantial estate to the Gallery. Another notable supporter was Isabel Pollard, a connoisseur and collector who became a life member of the Gallery. In 1961 she embarked on a long series of gifts of art works that was to make her the most notable and lavish benefactor to the Gallery's permanent collection.

Ina Uhthoff sacrificed vast amounts of time, which she might well have devoted to her professional career, in order to act as the

187

board's advisor on artistic matters. She was, in effect, chairperson of the exhibition committee. After 1950 she was aided in her devotion to the Gallery by her great personal friend, Hildegarde Wyllie, who continued to support the movement well into the 1960s. Another supporter on a broad scale was Miss Kathleen Agnew, who gave her spacious Rockland home on more than one occasion for money-raising ventures. It was typical of Miss Agnew that she gave to various organizations, in advance of her death, funds she was planning to bequeath in her will. On one auspicious day she distributed a total of $65,000, of which the Gallery received $5,000.

In 1947 the Little Centre "crowd," as they were usually referred to in City Hall council chambers, were greatly encouraged by the receipt of a grant of $500 from the council, and felt they had finally won official civic support. This proved to be the only grant from that source for years to come, however.

In May of that year the Plimley Company served notice that it would shortly terminate the Centre's lease. Thus the gallery organization and its eighty-eight members were out in the cold looking for new premises. During this interim period lectures were still sponsored and occasional shows continued to be mounted at Prince Robert House. Under the chairmanship of Lieutenant-Colonel E. H. Casper a search was begun once more for another temporary premises while storage was arranged for those furnishings and artifacts that the Little Centre had acquired. Everyone concerned was anxious but no one lost heart although it was some months before a solution appeared.

A new temporary home, at a rental of $75 dollars a month, was acquired in the Mellor Building (now the home of CFAX radio) on Broughton Street, just east of the Royal Theatre. Upon taking over this site the society dropped the word "Little," and "The Arts Centre of Greater Victoria" became its new title. The "Greater Victoria" part was inserted to nudge surrounding municipalities into realizing the Arts Centre was also serving their residents in addition to those of Victoria. Versatile architect John Wade created a simple but effective interior design for the bare-bones space using swags of inexpensive material and effective though not costly lighting arrangements.

The new Centre opened with an important show of drawings by then living British artists organized by the British Council and circulated across Canada by the National Gallery. In the spring of 1949 Victoria College's Dr. Harry Hickman succeeded Colonel Casper in the chair and instituted a vigorous programme of shows, lectures, films, and recorded concerts to satisfy the demands of the Centre's ever-increasing public.

In July, 1950, an important beginning was made towards the development of a permanent art collection. Mark Kearley wrote from Switzerland offering the gift of a fine large oil by the nineteenth century French painter Jean Monchablon in addition to several other minor works. Seven months later sisters Katherine and Alexandra McEwen, Anglo-Americans who had settled in Victoria during the war, added to these by donating several old master drawings and two imposing woodcuts by the eighteenth-century Japanese master Utamaro.

The Gallery members were kept occupied in various maintenance roles while enjoying a majority of the travelling shows that were available. Most were conscious that there were limitations with respect to what could be hung on the Gallery walls. A great many travelling shows were not available to the Arts Centre for security and insurance reasons. The most active members who would never accept as final a make-do situation continued to encourage the search for a permanent and viable gallery site. A leading businessman, G. A. Hebden, had taken on the chairmanship and under his guidance the search became more intense.

The Public Library Board rejected a proposal that a gallery space be built into the expanding premises on Blanshard and Yates Streets. The Provincial Secretary was approached in the hope that his government would provide the funds with which a gallery could be built. The response was that the provincial government was already planning to incorporate a gallery in the new museum it expected to erect. Unfortunately, only the museum was ever realized.

In 1951 Ina Uhthoff's staunch friend, Hildegarde Wyllie, became president. Wyllie had been in the chair only two months when she had the intense satisfaction of informing the board that she had a letter from Sara Spencer offering her family mansion at 1040 Moss Street "for purposes as an arts centre." The terms set forth in the letter appeared to make excellent sense from a business perspective: Miss Spencer stated that she wished her home to be owned by the city and to be operated as an arts centre by the Arts Centre board. After considering the terms the board saw no shoals ahead, only the relief of having ended the ceaseless hunt for a permanent, affordable site. Little did they know that the City Council hurdle would tax their own creative abilities.

Many board members felt that they lacked the experience, the wisdom, and the weight of some of the more prominent businessmen in the city in negotiating items such as this transfer of property. They therefore created an advisory board of notable Victorians on whom they might call for advice pertaining to major issues.

There were mixed reactions when the news of Miss Spencer's offer became public. The general feeling was that, for all its charm and spaciousness, the mansion offered a less than ideal solution to the problem of founding a civic gallery. One cautionary response proved to be far-seeing: the location lacked the advantage of being situated in a section of the city frequented by large numbers of passers-by, and, in addition, it was off the regular tourist routes. Against these objections it was argued that its peaceful and verdant setting provided a harmonious environment, matching the browsing mood of the gallery visitor.

Nevertheless, the possibility that the Centre would be offered an alternative anywhere near as generous and spacious as the Spencer mansion was to dream the impossible dream. The Moss Street site, as it turned out, was to experience rather the opposite of the nay-sayers' opinion. It proved almost from the beginning to be an extremely active arts centre, and within its first decade of operation was to enjoy the largest ratio of members to city population of any gallery in the country.

First the Centre had to deal with the stubborn parries and thrusts and the outright antagonism that boiled and sputtered among City Council. The board first made a modest proposal for a grant of $5,620 to operate the gallery from the Moss street location. Weeks and months passed as the council wrangled unceasingly. Eventually, particularly after the press became involved, the council reluctantly agreed to accept the Spencer offer but undertook only to provide $250 for the upkeep of the building exterior and to maintain the grounds up to an unspecified amount.

The next hurdle was the necessity of finding a knowledgeable person to direct proceedings of the Gallery — a curator. In Mrs. Uhthoff's thoughts there lingered on the image of a person who had taken watercolour lessons with her during a visit to Victoria, a young man of attractive personality, a west coaster by birth and choice, and who had a keen eye and an open mind where art was concerned. Thus Colin Graham, who had recently been lecturing at the California School of Fine arts in San Francisco, was appointed first curator.

It is impossible to overestimate the importance of Colin Graham's role in the development of the gallery. He was curator for twenty-two years and continued as director and director emeritus for another five. He and his wife, Sylvia, literally lived at the gallery for a few years, occupying a small apartment in the Spencer mansion in order to compensate somewhat for the low salary of $200 per month which was all the board could offer.

Graham seemed to work almost twenty-four hours a day. Apart entirely from the administrative duties and physical problems which had to be met, he had immediately to turn his attention to acquiring donations to the gallery which would lead to the development of a permanent collection. It was during his years as curator that the foundations for many of the gallery's most valuable collections were laid. It was also during his tenure that the two new wings were built, the Centennial gallery (including what would become the Graham gallery) in 1958 and the Ker Gallery in 1960.

One of Graham's great virtues was that he was tacful with everyone, even those people who had inherited Great Aunt Martha's watercolours and wanted to donate them to the gallery. His time was also taken up with people of leisure who had an interest in art, nothing to do, and found Graham an engaging companion. But cultivation of potential donors was essential and a large part of his time was invariably devoted to visiting people's houses to look at objets d'art or pictures, or in conducting interviews with potential benefactors.

Graham's experiences in creating one of the outstanding gallery's in Western Canada are too rich and varied to recount in detail here, but his reminiscences, "The Moss Street Years," should be required reading for anyone interested in arts development in this region.

In the mid-1950s something significant with respect to the visual arts occurred in the *Times* newsroom. My corner office had come to be regarded as the bureau through which many arts subjects were reported and discussed. For some time we had been offering our readers a weekly column dealing with the visual arts. We had been fairly fortunate in those who undertook the role of arts columnist and Colin Graham was one of the best of these. He knew his subject thoroughly and suited his vocabulary to the general readership. Others wrote for us as though addressing a learned body of arts specialists.

A recent art columnist belonged in that latter category but had left us for greener pastures, resulting in a gap with no one in sight to fill it — but not for long. One day when I was hard at work on a weekend feature I sensed a presence and looked up from my typewriter into the friendly smiling face of Moncrieff Williamson. It was friendship at first sight. He introduced himself, sat down, and told me that he had just come from Scotland. He had chosen Victoria as his destination because he had a relative in the city. He also told me, in a matter-of-fact way, that his speciality was art and provided me with an impressive background of his advanced education and achievement in the subject. I told him of our problem of adequately covering the comprehensive and growing fine arts activity in our city and suggested introducing him to our managing editor, Les Fox.

The introduction took place immediately and, without pause for pondering on either side, Moncrieff became our arts columnist that same day. He also became a lecturer in fine arts at UVIC and the part-time administrator of the Gallery's art classes and island extension services. He proved to be splendidly articulate and versatile in all areas — straightforward without arrogance, learned without hauteur, a man at ease with himself as he was with those around him. He left to become the full-time curator of the art department of Calgary's Glenbow Foundation and from there became the distinguished first director of the art gallery at Confederation Centre in Charlottetown. We knew we would lose him sooner or later but it was with selfish regret on our behalf that we eventually congratulated him and said goodbye.

In the early spring of 1973, a shock rang through Victoria when it was announced that Colin Graham would be retiring that August. When Richard Simmins came to take over Graham's position in September, Graham was asked to remain on the staff on a half-time basis. This he did for the next five years, maintaining close contact with the various donors who had become used to working with him, and helping to raise funds for the new Asian wing.

It was to be expected, with the advent of a new director, that there would be changes in some if not all aspects of the Gallery's operations. Although Richard Simmins's tenure was brief, his energetic and dynamic personality left a lasting impression. A creative thinker in the arts and a former director of the Vancouver Art Gallery, he turned his attention, with the help of financial resources then available from the federal government, to expanding the gallery's public offerings, changing its image, and bringing fresh audiences within reach of its collections.

In 1975 Simmins was succeeded by Roger Boulet, a young bilingual art historian from the National Gallery who remained for five years and took a particular interest in gallery publications. The original monthly newsletter to members had been changed to a newspaper-format magazine titled *De Cosmos* in Simmins' time. This was eventually superseded by *Arts Victoria*, a quality production with longer critical articles on collections and acquisitions than had been previously possible. It was edited by Robert Amos.

Although the basic aims of gallery policy during the years 1973–80 remained substantially the same as had been set up under Graham, there were varying shifts in emphases and implementation, a natural consequence of changes in personnel. It must be said, however, that even today there are Victorians who have never reconciled themselves to life at the gallery after 1973, expecting each of the three succeeding directors to be clones of Colin Graham.

Patricia Bovey, an art historian who had been curator of the Winnipeg Art Gallery, arrived in 1980 to replace Boulet. She arrived with a strong interest in community relations, so during the past 14 years there has been a continuous effort made not just to bring people of all ages and persuasions to the gallery, but to keep them there.

From its modest beginnings in Plimley's auto showroom, the gallery has grown to a large and complex organization with a staff of 31 in nine interlocking departments, a permanent collection worth approximately 30 million dollars, and a yearly budget of over 1.25 million. Even with these resources the Gallery could not operate without the assistance of hundreds of dedicated volunteers who back up the professional staff. More than half its revenue is self generating, the remainder coming from federal, provincial, municipal, corporate, and individual sources. Backing the entire organization is a Board of Trustees, which is ultimately responsible for policy decisions, with fifteen elected members and three sitting by virtue of their office. They quietly dedicate their time and effort to making sure that the Art Gallery of Greater Victoria survives.

The Gallery's present quarters, the Spencer mansion with the added modern wings, are now totally inadequate to contain and display its rich collections to advantage. It is not surprising, therefore, that the Board is currently considering a move to a new site large enough to contain a building specially designed to satisfy both present needs and those of the twentieth century.

☙

Epilogue

IFE in the newsroom had all begun for me in 1936 and it ended 51 years later in 1987. During those four decades I was to acquire a unique view of the Victoria arts scene. It was between those dates that Victoria commenced its remarkable growth and change of perspective. It started to develop a sense of the creative values inherent in the arts, to realize that change as well as permanence had value, and to finally leave behind the small-town perspective — the smug desire to keep things as they had been since the turn of the century.

Through the forties, fifties, and sixties a great deal of development took place in the expanding arts world of this off-centre city. Unquestionably there is no place like the desk of a newspaper arts columnist from which to observe what winds stirred among the trees and by whom they were channelled. As poet Adelaide Crapsey noted: "Is it as plainly in our living shown, by warp and twist which way the winds hath blown?"

Because I was fortunate enough (or determined enough) to have a seat "front row, centre" in all of these developments — not as a player, but as an observer — the story on the previous pages could be told. Not everybody has had the experience — nor would probably wish it — of talking for more than 50 years via printer's ink to an audience that can't interrupt, shout you down, or storm out of the room. There were dissidents, of course, who would either confront me or write irate letters to the editor, and certainly one or two angry and ambitious playwrights who accused me of being vicious and having destroyed them artistically and financially. But only one major eyeball-to-eyeball public encounter every took place.

There were a few truisms that I discovered in the first five challenging years, and one in particular — you can never stop learning. From the beginning I had the particular good fortune to cover a cross-section of all the performing arts, amateur and professional, in addition to working with editors who were encouraging and supportive. Boredom was something I naturally experienced from time to time but that was part of a job which also produced many high-lights and unexpected joys.

While my role in this drama has been satisfying it has not been without its "moments." Whatever one may call it — a job, a profession, a career, or a bloodless kind of mayhem — the critic's corner is contentious. Questions often asked of me in later years included: "How did you come to choose arts reporting as a career, of all things" or "How do you survive in such an ego-flattering but potentially dangerous occupation?" It was invariably implied that one had a strong streak of sadism or was a frustrated "wannabe" artist who gets satisfaction from tearing the wings off soaring talent.

The real joy, however, has been in watching the arts grow and develop in Victoria during, perhaps, its richest artistic period. Another satisfaction has involved the opportunity to write about these developments as they occurred — and, like George Dyke, get paid for it as well!

Index of Names

Abbott, Jocelyn, Norman, & Vivian 14, 74
Abbott, Margaret 87
Adamson, Anne 101, 122
Adaskin, Murray 68
Agnew, Kathleen 41, 188
Aitken, Robert 75
Alarie, Pierrette 75
Alexander, Viscount 186
Allen, Ralph 148, 151–59
Amos, Robert 194
Armstrong, Pat 165, 167, 174
Arngrim, Thor 120–21
Attrot, Ingrid 69
Austin, F. Victor 47
Austin, Karen 132
Austin, Pamela 187

Baird, Eva 39
Baird, Robert 135
Baker, Lloyd 34
Baker, Stuart 120
Ball, Michael 143
Balsom, Ed 26
Bantly, Benedict 37
Barraclough, Jack & Kay 55, 62, 64, 122
Bartalus, Ilona 68
Bates, Pat Martin 180
Beastall, Jack and Hilda 34
Beckow, Joan 166–67
Beckwith, Pamela (Terry) 79
Begbie, Sir Matthew Baillie 7
Bennett, Hon. & Mrs. W. A.C. 118
Bennett, Peter 143
Benson, Will. Jane, & Susan 150–51
Berrick, B. R. 186
Bishop, Roger 146, 160

Bladen, Ronald 185
Bo, Arne 57
Boer, Carole 173
Boulet, Roger 193
Bovey, Patricia 194
Bowers, Philip 87
Bray, John 81
Brett, Kathleen 93
Briggs, Vivian 126
Britt, John 88, b-vii
Brockington, Peter 133, 139, a-x
Broome, Edward 71
Brownsey, Richard 163
Bulley, Stanley 24–5, 38
Bullock-Webster 98, 100, 102
Bullock-Webster, Bill 17, 96, 99, 101–02, 105
Burnett, George Jennings 37
Burns, Flora Hamilton 179
Butchart, Jenny 54, 148
Butterfield, Benjamin 39
Byatt, Irene 39

Cameron, J. O. & Beatrix 40
Campbell, Aileen 32
Campbell, Graeme 144
Campbell, James 75
Campbell, Percy 71
Carr, Emily 127, 131, 179, 182, 185, 187
Casper, E. H. 188
Casson, Ann 142
Chadwick, Vivienne 119
Chambers, Coote Mulloy 47
Champion, Ruth 81, 90
Chamut, Bob 148
Chapple, Stanley 90
Chapple, Susan 139

Chow, Cary 74
Chubb, Frederick 37
Clack, Rod 133
Clack, Sam 50
Clay, Margaret 187
Coghill, Joy 132
Cole, Vincent 93
Cornish, Nellie 71
Costain, Dan 165, 173
Cothran, Robert 149, 156–58
Courtney, Richard 150–51
Cowan, Bunny (Hughes) 79
Cownden, Maurice 155
Crease, Josephine 182
Cridge, Edward 6
Curtis, Hugh 69
Cusack, Noel a-vii, a-viii

d'Arnould, Georges 47
Davies, Clem 123
Davis, Donald 169
Davis, Harry 106
de Turczynowicz, Laura 106
Deane-Drummond, Sophie 186 (see also Sophie Pemberton)
Denike, Howard 44, 89
Denton, Carl 71
Destrubé, Jean-Paul 174
Digby, Keith 141–42, 144
Dilworth, Ira 180
Donison, Chris 167
Donnelly, Denis 67
Dorrington, Charles 39, 90
Douglas, James 6
Douglas, Norma 43
Dowling, Judith 39, 86
Downes, Gwen 112, 119
Drean, John 88, b-vii
Droy, Jack 88
Dunbar, John "Jock" 39, 87, b-v
Duncan, Adeline 126
Duff, Eleanor 39, 81

Dunn, Alexander 68
Dunnet, David 44
Durand, Gertrude 67
Durand, Mrs. J. 65
Dyck, John 127–28, 129
Dyke, George J. 20–2, 24

Edgelow, Geoff 118
Edmond, Reby 99
English, J. F. K. & Ada 43–4, 54, 72–3, a-viii
Enns, Phillip 93
Evans, Dorothy (Hopgood) 44
Ewan, Gladys 187

Fahey, Winifred Lugrin 40, 80, 84
Fairbairn, Archie 98, a-iv
Fairfield, George 126
Fast, Glen 61
Feheregyhazi, Tibor 132
Field, Michael 140
Flatman, Barry 130
Forbes, Elizabeth 31–3
Fox, Les 31, 33–34, 193
Frampton, Percy 135
Franca, Celia 167
Fraser, Dougal 148
Freeman, Paul 59–60, 62
Frey, Paul 93
Frick, Kay 92

Gabora, Taras 75
Garvie, Peter 15–53, 155–56
Gaskell, Phyllis 136
Gati, Laszlo 58, 62, a-ii
Gayfer, James 126
George, Dan 160
George, Percy 109–10
Gillan, J. Q. 17
Gillespie. Mai (Mrs. Hebden) 41
Gimlour, Connie (see Connie Thompson)

Gislason, Garth 90
Goolden, Alixe (Mrs. Massy) 54–5,
  65
Gorrie, Colin & El;izabeth 135–36,
  172–75, 177, b-iii
Gosley, Jerry 126, 134, 173
Goult, John 88, 128
Goult, Adele (see Adele Lewis)
Graeme, John 67
Graham, Colin 190–93, b-ix
Graves, Warren 143
Green, Gertrude Huntly (Mrs. J.
  Drand) 13, 40, 47, 65, a-vi
Grimshaw, Barry 88
Groos, Madelaine 84
Gruber, Hans 54–5, 62, 64, a-vi
Gruber June (Milburn) 87

Haddaway, Jean (Harness) 79
Haddock, Courtney 135
Hall, Margaret 126, 148
Hamilton, Malcolm 53
Hanby, Jackson 37
Hannigan, Beth 157
Hare, Carl 126, 147–48, 156, 158–
  60, 163
Harness, Jean (see Jean Haddaway)
Harris, Anne 87
Hart, Eva (Mrs. J. Q. Gillan) 17, 39
Hartie, R. 50
Heath, John 88, 136, 138, b-viii
Hebden, G. A. 188
Heffelfinger, George & Jane 91–2
Helmcken, John Sebastian 40
Helmcken, Mrs. James Douglas 40
Hembroff, Edythe 182
Henderson, Hugh 177, a-xii
Hendry, Lynn 74
Heslup, Willie 159
Hickman, Harry 189
Hicks, Gideon 37
Hilker, Gordon 40

Himmick, Michelle 74
Hincks, Reginald 16
Hirsch, John 121
Hoban, Stanley 84, b-iv
Hobbs, Isabel 186
Hobbs, Marguerite 87
Hodgson, Alan 122
Hogya, Giles 111, 166–67, 174
Holliston, Robert 14
Holmes, Cuthbert 187
Hood, Dawn 90
Horsfall, Basil & Elfrida 77–8, 106
Horthy, Carl (Douglas C. Horth) 78
Hosie, Bill & Sylvia 136, 165
House, Dorothea 136
Howard, Kay 132
Hughes, Gwynedd & Norah 79, 88
  (see also Bunny Cowan)
Humphreys, Sidney 45, 66, 68, a-v
Humphreys, Smyth 66
Hunter, James 45, 68, a-v
Hurn, H. S. "Bunny" 102, 105, 109
Hyland, Frances 143, 158, 169

Isherwood, Foster 148

James, Leonard 7
James, Selena 69, 90
Jenkins, Anthony 132, 148, a-ix
Johannesen, J. J. 74, 76
Johns, Harry & Thelma 39, 79, 84,
  b-iv
Johnson, Maurice 26–7, 31, 82–3,
  87, 113–15, 122, 154, 177
Jones, Tudor 89

Karr, Gary 75
Keane, John 114–15, a-viii
Kearley, Mark 101, 185–87, 189
Keate, Stuart 31, 33, 56
Keen, Charles 7
Kent, Denis & Douglas 49–50

Kessler, Jack 68
King, Frederic 38
Knight, Elizabeth (Mrs. Betty Mayne) 118
Knudsen, Melvin 50–1, 53, 79
Kotanen, Ed 140
Kramer, Karen 173
Krich, John 111, 159, b-i, b-ii
Kwok, May-Ling 14, 74
Kyle, John 184

Lambertson, Chet 148
Lanchester, Elsa 125
Langdale, Stella 187
Langford, Edward Edwards 6
Leard, Jim 177
LeBel, Pauline 167
Lester, Alan 160
Lewis, Adele 39, 81, 87, b-v, b-vi
Lewis, Catherine 39
Leyshon, Glynis 91, 138, 162–3, 170, a-v
Liittich, Paul 173–74, 177
Lister, Fraser 79
Litt, Richard & Sheila 88, b-vii

McCabe, Robin 75
McCarthy, Sheila 165
McClure, Samuel 7
McCoppin, Peter 61
MacCorkindale, Archie 99
MacDonald, Dan 131
Macdonald, Eric 140
MacDonald, Ken 165, 167
McEwen, Katherine & Alexandra 189
McIntyre, Barbara 156–57, 159–60
McIntyre, Ian 136
McKenzie, Ron 128
MacLaughlin, Barbara 173
McLeod, Gordon 104
McManus, Don 132–33, 136

McMillan, Sir Ernest 54
MacMillan, Norma 120–21
McPherson, Thomas S. 121, 124, 127
McQueen, Jim 139
McSween, Wally 142
McVie, James 79

Maltwood, John 184–5
Mannering, Peter 120–22, 124, 130–31, 133–36, a-viii, a-x
Margison, Gilbert 49
Margison, Richard 49, 69, 74, 144, b-ix
Martin, Margaret 127, 136, 144
Martin, Stanley 84
Martin, Warren 50
Massam, George 88
Maxwell, Andrew 63
Mayeska, Irene 139
Mayhew, Elza 52
Maynard, Max 181
Mayne, Betty (Elizabeth Knight) 119
Meiklejohn, Michæl 88, b-vii
Menelaws, Will 181, 186
Merriman, Tom 33–4
Michaux, Emil 44
Milburn, June (see June Gruber)
Montgomery, Robert 165
Moon, Pieranne 68
Morgan, Graham 71
Morris, Michael 180
Mueller, Otto-Werner 55, 57–8, 64, 66, 126–27
Mulliner, Betty 49
Mylam, Nellie Ella 9–12

Netherton, Jim 173
Neville, John 141
Newcombe, W. J. B. 187, 179
Newton, Christopher 92
Nichol, Eric 131

200

Nichol, Quita (Mrs. Walter) 41
Nicholson, Flora 104

Ockenden, Fay & Helen 49, 51
Odinsky, Fran 141
Oldham, David 79
Ord, Mrs. Wilfrid & Clemency 40
O'Reilly, Mary 114

Packard, Peggy Walton 39, 84, 87,
    131, b-iv, b-v, b-vi, b-ix
Packard, Wendy (Mrs. Timothy
    Vernon) 131
Painter, Lincoln 87
Palmer, David 84
Parker, G. H. 186
Parlow, Kathleen 40
Partridge, Bruce 155
Pavelic, Myfanwy 51, 181
Payne, Sam 120, 127, 134, a-x
Peacock, David 139, 176
Pearce, Mary 186
Pearse, Benjamin W. 6
Pemberton, Augustus 6
Pemberton, Sophie 180–81 (see also
    Sophie Deane-Drummond)
Petch, Ernie 17
Pfau, Monica 74
Pferdner, Emile 47
Phillips, Robin 164
Pickett, Hugh 40
Plimley, Thomas 186
Poggemiller, Barbara 173
Pollard, Isabel 187
Pollen, Peter 135
Pollet, Frances 85
Polson, Arthur 68
Poole, Ian 139
Potter, Miles 170
Prescott, Alfred 49, 51
Price, Robert 148
Privett, Molly 187

Prossnitz, Walter 14, 74
Proudman, Richard 81, 83–4
Pryce, Drury 47–8
Purdy, Allan 88–9, 110, 122, 128,
    b-vii, b-ix
Purves-Hume, Gina 165

Quilico, Louis 56

Rain, Douglas 140, a-xi
Rattenbury, Francis Mawson 7
Reed, Dale 68
Reed, Gordon 165
Reiser, Alan 74
Risk, Sydney 114
Ross, Christopher 148
Ross, Ian and Ann-Lee 54
Roy, James 169

Sabiston, Andrew 131, a-xi
Sabiston, Carole 90, 92, 131, 157
Scott, Gwen 187
Scott, Mary-Jane 111
Scott, Pat 148
Scott, Winifred 66 (see also Mrs.
    Robin Wood)
Sehl, Frank 47
Sekiya, Yukio 177
Senior, Janet 89
Sexton, Very Rev. H. E. 82
Shadbolt, Jack 181–82
Shale, Stanley 11, 13, 65, a-vi
Shaw, Wynne 126
Shipley 165
Shipley, Don 164–66 169–70
Shore, Catherine 84
Shu-Qi, Chang 186
Siebner, Herbert 181
Siegrist, Hans 68
Simmins, Richard 193
Simon, Jack 92, 139, 158, 174
Simoneau, Léopold 75

Simpson-Baikie, Helen 131, 133, 135–36, 172
Sinclair, Lister 114
Skinner, Colin 90
Smith, Helen 111, 115, 148, a-viii
Smith, Peter 147–48
Solose, Katherine 68
Somerset, Dorothy 114
Sparling, Sydney 87
Spencer, Fred 111–12
Spencer, Sara 50–1, 54, 181, 187, 190
Spencer, Will 51
Stanick, Gerald 75
Stark, Barbara (Gurney) 79
Steed, Graham 38–9, a-ix
Steffan, Hans 87, b-vi
Stenner, Walter 54
Stephen, Hugh 67, 132
Stephen, Michael 163
Stephenson, Edwin 131, 134, 135, 137, 139–41, 172, a-xii
Stichbury, Allan 159
Swinton, Mary 165

Taylor, Harold 43, 48
Taylor, Malcolm 44, 146
Temple, Judy 68, 90
Terry, Pamela (see Mrs. John Beckwith)
Thompson, Connie (Gilmour) 99
Thorne, Ian 117–18, 120
Timp, Pierre 39
Topham, Jean 87
Treloar, Judy 111
Tremayne, W. A. 78
Trueman, Jack 132, 139, 140
Turgeon, C. J. 186
Turner, Louis 47
Tweten, Bob 74

Tyrrell, Norman 39, 81, 84, 87, b-iv, b-v, b-vi
Tyrwhitt-Drake, Constance 39, 41–2

Uhthoff, Ina 15, 180–83, 186–88, 190–91
Ulrich, Ron 139

Vernon, Timothy 91, 94, 126, 131, b-iv, b-x

Wade, John 189
Ward, Robert 106
Warren, Michael 148
Waters, Maryla 140, a-xii
Watkis, Frank 47
Watt, Georgina (Hobbis) 38
Watts, Mollie 42
Way, Ron 88
Webb, Gerald 88, b-vii
Webb, Kate 9–10, 12–3
Webb, Ron 88
Webster, Rodney 68
Weir, G. M. 97
West, Bill 92, 157, 159, b-x
Whitlow, Very Rev. Brian 81, 83, 87
Wickett, Dudley 37
Wiebe, Arthur 39
Willett, Wilfred 48
Williamson, Moncrieff 192
Wills, Archie 22, 24, 28, 30–1
Wilson, Lily 39
Wood, Roberto & Mary 37, 72
Wood, Robin & Winifred 14, 44–5, 66–7, a-iv, a-v
Wyllie, Hildegarde 188, 190

Young, Catherine 68, 89
Young, E. V. 79